Contents

About *Hands-On Science*...3

Teaching Tips...4

Getting Started 5

National Science Education Standards..................6

Science Process Skills 7

Hands-On Science Themes

Aquarium *Life Science)*..8

Students observe interactions between organisms and their environment in an aquarium ecosystem.

Sound *Physical Science)* 18

Students recognize that sound is produced by vibrations and experiment with volume and pitch.

Sun and Shadows *Earth Science)*..................................28

Students experiment with shadows, recognizing how they form and change shape.

Nutrition *Life Science)*..38

Students conduct tests on various foods to determine their nutritional value.

Cold and Heat *(Physical Science)* 48

Students demonstrate how heat moves and experiment with variables that affect the movement of heat.

Air *Earth and Physical Science)*.....................................58

Students identify some of the different properties of air, as well as some of its uses.

Bubbles *Physical Science)* 68

Students experiment with bubble shape, interactions between bubbles, and bubble refraction of light.

My Five Senses *(Life Science)* 78

Students perform a variety of experiments that make use of their different senses.

Sink and Float *Physical Science)* 88

Students recognize what makes an object sink or float and experiment with variables that determine an object's tendency to sink or float.

Animal Behavior *Life Science)* 98

Students gather data on the behavior of mealworms and snails and relate the behavior to each organism's survival strategy.

Water *(Earth Science)* 108

Students experiment to determine some of the physical properties of water and components of the water cycle.

Magnets *Physical Science)* 118

Students observe interactions between magnets and magnetic objects, experiment with like and unlike poles, and create a temporary magnet.

Plants *Life Science)* 128

Students investigate variables that affect the health of plants and identify some of the needs of plants.

Color *Physical Science)* 138

Students experiment with color pigments, color filters, and color mixing.

Life Cycles *Life Science)* 148

Students observe the life cycles of garden pea plants and mealworms.

Rocks and Soil *Earth Science)* 158

Students observe different rocks and soil types and make inferences about how soil is formed.

Light *Physical Science)* 168

Students experiment with reflection, refraction, lenses, and the visible light spectrum.

Weather *(Earth Science)* 178

Students use tools to collect and record weather data over a period of time.

Chemistry *Physical Science)* 188

Students experiment with different chemicals, observing a number of physical and chemical changes.

Microorganisms *Life Science)* 198

Students culture a variety of microorganisms and recognize both their helpful and harmful influences.

About Hands-On Science

Each of the 20 hands-on units includes the following sections:

Teacher resource pages

objectives

materials list

preparation

background information

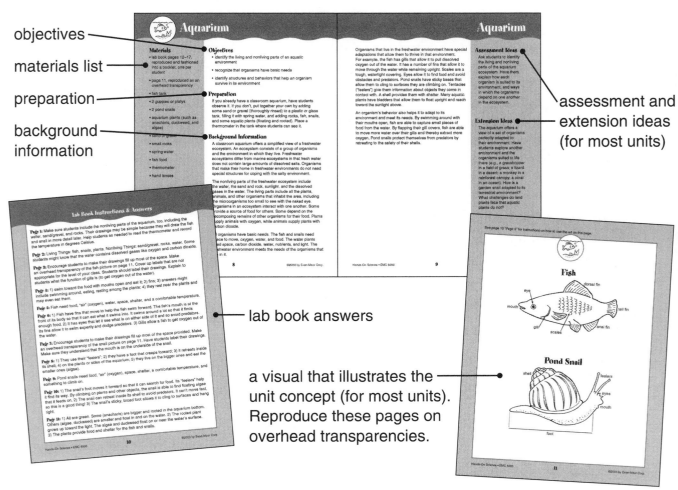

assessment and extension ideas (for most units)

lab book answers

a visual that illustrates the unit concept (for most units). Reproduce these pages on overhead transparencies.

Student lab book pages

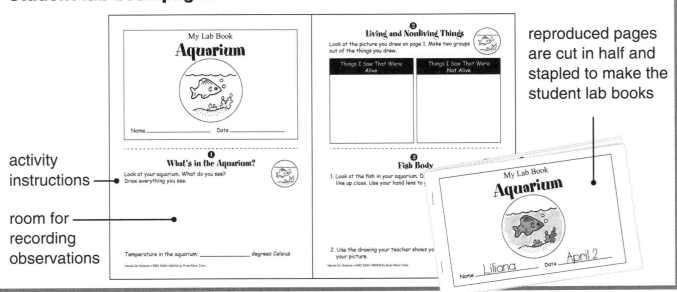

activity instructions

room for recording observations

reproduced pages are cut in half and stapled to make the student lab books

Scheduling and Organization

- Each unit contains a number of exercises for students to perform. You may choose to have students complete one or more lab book pages in a day. The pace you follow is up to you.

- Some of the activities can be performed by students working alone. Others would be better performed in small groups, especially those that require materials. Before students begin working on an exercise, decide whether they will work alone, with a partner, or with a group.

- Hands-on experience is always better than simple observation, so try to have students perform as many of the experiments as possible. You might want to recruit adult volunteers to help student groups as they work on their experiments.

Working with Younger Students

Students are asked to record their observations and conclusions on the pages of their lab books. If your students are emergent or beginning writers, you may choose to use the lab books to simply guide the investigation along. Students can share their observations and conclusions verbally rather than writing them out. Younger students can still use the back of the lab book pages to draw what happened in their experiments.

Managing Materials

Follow these ideas for making cleanup as easy as possible:

- In experiments using water or other liquids, have students cover their work areas with newspaper to absorb spills.

- Keep plenty of paper towels handy for spills and other messes.

- Set up "Distribution Stations" for students to collect bulk materials they might need during an experiment (such as salt, water, sugar, and so on).

- Designate a "Materials Area" to store materials that will be used in more than one exercise.

- Go over experiment and cleanup procedures with students before you begin an experiment.

Safety

Safety is always a top concern when conducting science experiments with young children. Go over the safety rules of the science lab with your students before beginning any experiment. Remind students never to eat or drink anything in science lab unless instructed to do so by you.

Getting Started

To prepare for each unit, follow these simple steps:

1. Read both the teacher information pages and the student lab book sheets.

2. Photocopy the pages of the student lab book. Cut the lab book pages and staple them on one side to form a booklet. Prepare one booklet for each student.

3. Decide which page(s) of the unit you would like students to complete each day.

4. Collect the materials needed to complete the pages you selected. For some exercises, students will be working on their own. For others, you may choose to break students into small groups and have them share materials.

5. Where applicable, try out the exercises covered in the pages to familiarize yourself with the procedure and expected result.

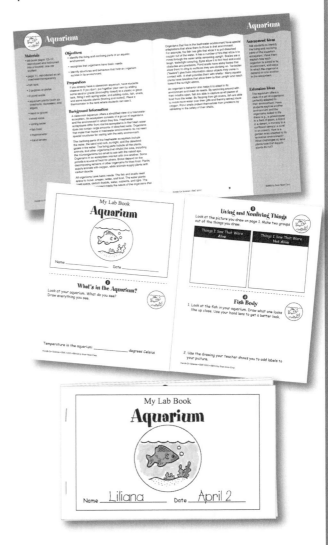

Lab Book Answers

Students may come up with responses that are different from those provided on the teacher page. These responses may be equally valid. Judge each answer according to how carefully observations were made and recorded.

Storing Lab Books

Decide on a place to store the lab books. Pass out students' lab books at the beginning of each experiment and return them to the storage area at the end. The books will allow you and the students to keep track of the work they have completed. Once units are completed, students can take their books home and share their work with their families.

The *National Science Education Standards* (National Academy Press, 1996) outlines what students need to know, understand, and be able to do to be "scientifically literate." What does it mean to be scientifically literate? It means being able to use scientific information to make choices and engage intelligently in public debate about important issues that involve science and technology.

Content Standards for Grades K–4

The *Standards* states that as a result of activities, students should develop an understanding of the following content:

Physical Science

Properties of objects and materials
Position and motion of objects
Light, heat, electricity, and magnetism

Life Science

Characteristics of organisms
Life cycles of organisms
Organisms and environments

Earth and Space Science

Properties of earth materials
Objects in the sky
Changes in earth and sky

Experiments in *Hands-On Science* cover each of the content areas listed above.

Scientific Inquiry

The *Standards* states that as a result of activities in grades K–4, all students should develop

• the abilities necessary to do scientific inquiry and

• an understanding about scientific inquiry.

Younger students should be developing their abilities to do science and their understanding of science in accordance with their developmental capabilities. This means understanding the process of investigation, learning how to ask scientific questions, making careful observations, using evidence to construct reasonable explanations, and communicating results to others. Experiments in *Hands-On Science* promote the development of these skills.

Science Process Skills

As part of the process of scientific inquiry, students are expected to develop and apply the following science process skills. Student lab books encourage students to use these skills as they complete each unit.

Observing

Observation is the use of one or more of the five senses to describe the properties of objects or events. Observation should be as objective as possible, without the influence of opinion or "feeling."

Measuring

A measurement is the determination of a physical characteristic of an object as compared to a standard. Measurements include physical dimensions, mass, quantity, duration, and so on. Students should learn how to use tools associated with taking measurements, including rulers, scales, and stopwatches.

Predicting

A prediction is a projection about what might happen in the future based on evidence from observations of past events. A prediction is always based on evidence and is never simply a "guess."

Inferring

An inference is an explanation or prediction based indirectly on evidence. For example, evidence from one situation can be applied to another hypothetical situation to explain what might happen there.

Recording

Observations, data, and analyses must be recorded clearly and accurately in a journal so that the information can be shared with others.

Aquarium

Materials

- lab book pages 12–17, reproduced and fashioned into a booklet, one per student
- page 11, reproduced as an overhead transparency
- fish tank
- 2 guppies or platys
- 2 pond snails
- aquarium plants (such as anacharis, duckweed, and algae)
- sand or gravel
- small rocks
- spring water
- fish food
- thermometer
- hand lenses

Objectives

- identify the living and nonliving parts of an aquatic environment
- recognize that organisms have basic needs
- identify structures and behaviors that help an organism survive in its environment

Preparation

If you already have a classroom aquarium, have students observe it. If you don't, put together your own by adding some sand or gravel (thoroughly rinsed) to a plastic or glass tank, filling it with spring water, and adding rocks, fish, snails, and some aquatic plants (floating and rooted). Place a thermometer in the tank where students can see it.

Background Information

A classroom aquarium offers a simplified view of a freshwater ecosystem. An ecosystem consists of a group of organisms and the environment in which they live. Freshwater ecosystems differ from marine ecosystems in that fresh water does not contain large amounts of dissolved salts. Organisms that make their home in freshwater environments do not need special structures for coping with the salty environment.

The nonliving parts of the freshwater ecosystem include the water, the sand and rock, sunlight, and the dissolved gases in the water. The living parts include all the plants, animals, and other organisms that inhabit the area, including the microorganisms too small to see with the naked eye. Organisms in an ecosystem interact with one another. Some provide a source of food for others. Some depend on the decomposing remains of other organisms for their food. Plants supply animals with oxygen, while animals supply plants with carbon dioxide.

All organisms have basic needs. The fish and snails need space to move, oxygen, water, and food. The water plants need space, carbon dioxide, water, nutrients, and light. The freshwater environment meets the needs of the organisms that live in it.

Organisms that live in the freshwater environment have special adaptations that allow them to thrive in that environment. For example, the fish has gills that allow it to pull dissolved oxygen out of the water. It has a number of fins that allow it to move through the water while remaining upright. Scales are a tough, watertight covering. Eyes allow it to find food and avoid obstacles and predators. Pond snails have sticky bases that allow them to cling to surfaces they are climbing on. Tentacles ("feelers") give them information about objects they come in contact with. A shell provides them with shelter. Many aquatic plants have bladders that allow them to float upright and reach toward the sunlight above.

An organism's behavior also helps it to adapt to its environment and meet its needs. By swimming around with their mouths open, fish are able to capture small pieces of food from the water. By flapping their gill covers, fish are able to move more water over their gills and thereby extract more oxygen. Pond snails protect themselves from predators by retreating to the safety of their shells.

Assessment Ideas

Ask students to identify the living and nonliving parts of the aquarium ecosystem. Have them explain how each organism is suited to its environment, and ways in which the organisms depend on one another in the ecosystem.

Extension Ideas

The aquarium offers a view of a set of organisms perfectly adapted to their environment. Have students explore another environment and the organisms suited to life there (e.g., a grasshopper in a field of grass; a lizard in a desert; a monkey in a rainforest canopy; a coral in an ocean). How is a garden snail adapted to its terrestrial environment? What challenges do land plants face that aquatic plants do not?

Lab Book Instructions & Answers

Page 1: Make sure students include the nonliving parts of the aquarium, too, including the water, sand/gravel, and rocks. Their drawings may be simple because they will draw the fish and snail in more detail later. Help students as needed to read the thermometer and record the temperature in degrees Celsius.

Page 2: Living Things: fish, snails, plants. Nonliving Things: sand/gravel, rocks, water. Some students might know that the water contains dissolved gases like oxygen and carbon dioxide.

Page 3: Encourage students to make their drawings fill up most of the space. Make an overhead transparency of the fish picture on page 11. Cover up labels that are not appropriate for the level of your class. Students should label their drawings. Explain to students what the function of gills is (to get oxygen out of the water).

Page 4: 1) swim toward the food with mouths open and eat it; 2) fins; 3) answers might include swimming around, eating, resting among the plants; 4) they rest near the plants and may even eat them.

Page 5: Fish need food, "air" (oxygen), water, space, shelter, and a comfortable temperature.

Page 6: 1) Fish have fins that move to help the fish swim forward. The fish's mouth is at the front of its body so that it can eat what it swims into. It swims around a lot so that it finds enough food. 2) It has eyes that let it see what is on either side of it and so avoid predators. Its fins allow it to swim expertly and dodge predators. 3) Gills allow a fish to get oxygen out of the water.

Page 7: Encourage students to make their drawings fill up most of the space provided. Make an overhead transparency of the snail picture on page 11. Have students label their drawings. Make sure they understand that the mouth is on the underside of the snail.

Page 8: 1) They use their "feelers"; 2) they have a foot that creeps forward; 3) it retreats inside its shell; 4) on the plants or sides of the aquarium; 5) they live on the bigger ones and eat the smaller ones (algae).

Page 9: Pond snails need food, "air" (oxygen), space, shelter, a comfortable temperature, and something to climb on.

Page 10: 1) The snail's foot moves it forward so that it can search for food. Its "feelers" help it find its way. By climbing on plants and other objects, the snail is able to find floating algae that it feeds on. 2) The snail can retreat inside its shell to avoid predators. It can't move fast, so this is a good thing! 3) The snail's sticky, broad foot allows it to cling to surfaces and hang tight.

Page 11: 1) All are green. Some (anacharis) are bigger and rooted in the aquarium bottom. Others (algae, duckweed) are smaller and float in and on the water. 2) The rooted plant grows up toward the light. The algae and duckweed float on or near the water's surface. 3) The plants provide food and shelter for the fish and snails.

Fish

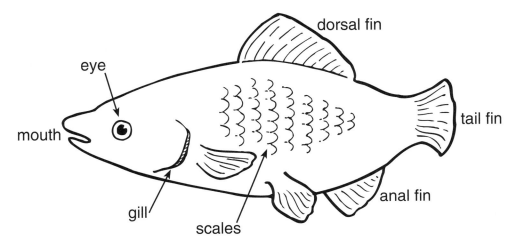

Pond Snail

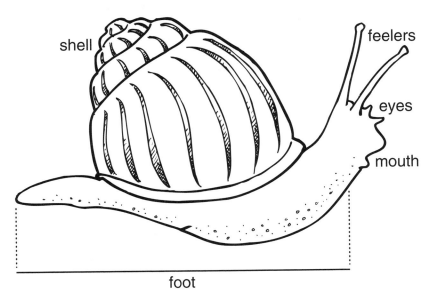

My Lab Book

Aquarium

Name _____   Date _____

- -

❶
What's in the Aquarium?

Look at your aquarium. What do you see?
Draw everything you see.

Temperature in the aquarium: _____ degrees Celsius

Hands-On Science • EMC 5000 • ©2003 by Evan-Moor Corp.

❷ Living and Nonliving Things

Look at the picture you drew on page 1. Make two groups out of the things you drew.

Things I Saw That Were Alive	Things I Saw That Were Not Alive

- -

❸ Fish Body

1. Look at the fish in your aquarium. Draw what one looks like up close. Use your hand lens to get a better look.

2. Use the drawing your teacher shows you to add labels to your picture.

❹ Fish Behavior

1. Sprinkle some fish food in the aquarium. What do the fish do?

_____

2. What body parts help the fish swim?

_____

3. What do the fish spend most of their time doing?

_____

_____

4. How do the fish interact with the plants in the aquarium?

_____

_____

- -

❺ What Fish Need

What do you think fish need to live in the aquarium?
(Hint: Think about what you need to live. Fish might need
some of the same kinds of things.)

_____

_____

_____

_____

_____

❻ How Fish Meet Their Needs

1. Look at the picture of the fish you drew on page 3. How does a fish's body and behavior help it get food?

_____

_____

2. How do a fish's body and behavior help it get away from other bigger fish that might want to eat it?

_____

_____

3. How does a fish's body help it get oxygen from the water?

_____

_____

- -

❼ Snail Body

1. Look at the pond snails in your aquarium. Draw what one looks like up close. What parts can you see with the hand lens?

2. Use the drawing your teacher shows you to add labels to your picture.

❽
Snail Behavior

1. How do the pond snails find out what is around them?

_____

2. How do pond snails move?

_____

3. What does a pond snail do when it is bothered?

_____

4. Where do the snails spend most of their time?

_____

5. How do the snails interact with the plants in the aquarium?

_____

- -

❾
What Snails Need

What do you think pond snails need to live in the aquarium?
(Hint: Think about what you need to live. Pond snails might
need some of the same kinds of things.)

_____

_____

_____

_____

_____

⑩
How Snails Meet Their Needs

1. Look at the picture of the pond snail you drew on page 7. How does a pond snail's body and behavior help it get food?

_____

_____

2. How do a pond snail's body and behavior help it get away from other animals that might want to eat it?

_____

_____

3. How does a pond snail's body help it climb up plants?

_____

_____

- -

⑪
Aquarium Plants

1. Look at the plants in your aquarium. How are they alike? How are they different from each other?

_____

_____

2. Plants need light to grow. How does the location of the plants help them to get enough light?

_____

_____

3. How do the plants help the animals in the aquarium?

_____

Sound

Materials

- lab book pages 22–27, reproduced and fashioned into a booklet, one per student
- page 21, reproduced as an overhead transparency
- cups, paper or foam
- rubber bands
- glass bottles
- pencils
- wooden rulers
- paper plates
- rice
- radio
- string
- paper clips
- water
- scissors

Objectives

- identify a variety of sounds and infer how they are made
- recognize that vibrations produce sounds
- observe that sound travels through solids as well as gases
- experiment with volume and pitch
- apply knowledge of pitch to create a tune

Preparation

Label six identical glass soda bottles with the numbers 1 through 6. Add a different amount of water to each bottle, as follows:

Bottle Number	Amount Filled
1	$\frac{1}{6}$
2	$\frac{1}{3}$
3	$\frac{1}{2}$
4	$\frac{2}{3}$
5	$\frac{5}{6}$
6	full

Prepare as many sets of bottles as possible so that students can work in small groups. Alternatively, you may choose to have small groups of students take turns using the one set.

Make arrangements to bring a radio into the classroom for the activity on lab book page 24. The more radios you have, the smaller the student groups can be. The radio(s) must be large enough to set a paper plate on.

Cut the string into lengths of 5 feet, one per pair of students.

Background Information

Sound is created when a vibrating object creates sound waves. These sound waves move away from the vibrating object in all directions. When the sound waves strike our eardrums, a message is sent to our brains, and we hear sound.

Sound waves are mechanical waves, that is, they need a medium to travel through. That medium can be a gas (like air), a liquid (like water in a pool), or a solid (like a table). Sound cannot travel through a vacuum (a space with no air). This is why we can't hear sound in space.

Sounds can be made by striking an object (percussion), plucking strings (stringed instruments), and by blowing air across an opening (wind instruments). Each action causes a vibration, which produces sound. The human voice is created by passing air over a set of vocal cords in the throat area that vibrate to produce different sounds.

The volume of a sound, how loud or soft it is, depends on how much energy went into creating it. Loud sounds have large amplitudes and carry a lot of energy. Soft sounds have small amplitudes and carry less energy. You can vary the volume of a sound by varying how much energy is used to create it.

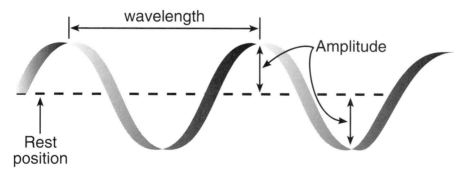

The pitch of a sound, or how high or low it is, depends on the rate of vibration of the wave. Higher pitched sounds have a greater frequency than sounds with lower pitches. (Frequency is a measure of how many waves are produced per second. The higher the frequency of a wave, the shorter the wavelength.) You can vary the pitch of a sound by varying the rate of vibration of the object that produced it.

Assessment Ideas

Ask students to explain what all sounds have in common. (They are all produced by vibrations.) Ask them to identify as many materials as they can that sound moves through (e.g., air, walls, telephone wires, string, bottles, water). Have them test some of their ideas.

Extension Ideas

Bring a collection of musical instruments into the classroom for students to examine. (Your school music department may have some you can borrow.) Allow students to experiment with the instruments. Then ask them to pick their favorite one and identify how it produces sound.

Page 1: Student answers might include the sound of a dog barking, a garbage truck backing up, the wind moving through the leaves of a tree, water running in a stream, voices talking, and so on.

Page 2: Students will need a cup, a rubber band, a pencil, and a glass bottle. Student ideas might include tapping the cup with the pencil, tapping the bottle with the pencil, stretching the rubber band between their fingers and plucking it, and so on.

Page 3: Students will need a wooden ruler. 2) nothing; 3) a "twanging" sound; 4) the ruler is vibrating back and forth.

Page 4: Students will need a rubber band and a cup. 2) nothing; 3) a "twanging" sound; 4) It is vibrating.

Page 5: Students will need a paper plate, some rice grains, and a radio. 2) it begins to "dance"; 3) the radio is vibrating; 4) the vibrating radio makes the rice start dancing; 5) it will stop dancing. Encourage students to test their predictions.

Page 6: 1) nothing; 2) vibrations; 3) more vibrations; 4) they all vibrate.

Page 7: 2) faint sound; 4) the sound is louder with my ear on the desk; 5) through the table.

Page 8: Students will need a paper cup and a 5-foot length of string (one per team). Show students how to use a pencil to poke a small hole in the bottom of their cups, pass the end of the string through the hole, and use a paper clip to secure it inside the bottom. 2) muffled sound; 4) students should be able to hear what their partner is saying; 5) through the string.

Page 9: Students will need a cup and a rubber band. 1) tap-tap; 2) by hitting the desk more lightly; 3) a "twanging" sound; 4) by plucking the rubber band harder.

Page 10: Students will need a set of six prepared bottles and a pencil. 2) bottle #1; 3) bottle #6; 4) yes; 5) lower.

Page 11: Students will need a set of bottles and a pencil. Make an overhead transparency of the pattern on page 21. The numbers correspond to the bottle numbers. Students should tap each bottle as indicated in order to produce the tune "Mary Had a Little Lamb."

Name This Tune

③ ④ ⑤ ④ ③ ③ ③

④ ④ ④ ③ ② ②

③ ④ ⑤ ④ ③ ③ ③ ③

④ ④ ③ ④ ⑤

21

My Lab Book
Sound

Name _____ Date _____

- -

❶
Different Sounds

Think about some of the different sounds you hear every day. Write them below. Then explain how each sound is made.

	Sound and How It Is Made
1	
2	
3	
4	
5	

❷
How to Make Sounds

How many different sounds can you make using a cup, a rubber band, a pencil, and a bottle? Describe what materials you used and what you did with them.

Sound	Materials Used	What I Did with Them

- -

❸
Good Vibrations

1. Lay a wooden ruler on the edge of your desk. Hold the end down with your hand. Most of it should hang over the edge.

2. Press down hard on the other end of the ruler and then let go.

3. What did you hear?

_____

_____

4. What did you see?

_____

❹ Rubber Band Guitar

1. Stretch a rubber band around a cup from top to bottom.

2. Put your ear near the cup. What do you hear?

_____

3. Next, pluck the rubber band with your finger. What do you hear?

_____

4. Pluck the rubber band again. Look closely at it as it makes a sound. What do you notice about the rubber band?

_____

- -

❺ Rockin' Rice

1. Put rice on a paper plate. Place the plate on the radio.

2. Turn on the radio. What happens to the rice?

_____

3. Touch the side of the radio. What do you feel?

_____

4. What do you think makes the rice do what it does?

_____

5. Make a prediction: If you turn off the radio, what will happen to the rice?

_____

❻ Vocal Vibrations

1. Place your hand on your throat. Don't talk. What do you feel?

_____

2. Now start humming. What do you feel?

_____

3. Now start talking. What do you feel?

_____

4. What do your throat, the ruler, the rubber band, and the radio all have in common when they are making sounds?

_____

_____

- -

❼ How Sound Travels

1. Pick a partner. Sit at your desk. Have your partner tap lightly on your desk.

2. Describe what you hear.

3. Now lay your ear against the top of your desk. Have your partner tap again lightly.

4. Compare this sound to the sound you heard before you put your ear on the desk. Which is louder?

_____

5. Does sound travel better through air or through the table?

_____

⑧ String Telephone

1. Pick a partner. Stand about 5 feet apart.

2. Hold a paper cup to your mouth and talk into it. Have your partner do the same. What do you hear?

_____

3. Now connect a piece of string between your cup and your partner's cup. Your teacher will show you how.

4. Hold the cup up to your ear. Have your partner talk into his or her cup. What do you hear?

_____

5. How did the sound travel to your ear?

_____

- -

⑨ Loud or Soft?

1. Tap a pencil against your desk. Describe the sound it makes.

_____

2. How can you make the same sound, but softer?

_____

3. Stretch a rubber band around a cup like you did before. Pluck the string. Describe the sound the rubber band makes.

_____

4. How can you make the same sound, but louder?

_____

⑩ High or Low?

1. Look at the six bottles of water. Blow across the top of each one.

2. Which one made the highest sound?

_____

3. Which one made the lowest sound?

_____

4. Now tap the bottles with a pencil. Did you get the same results?

_____

5. Circle the correct answer:

   The more water in the bottle, the lower/higher
   the sound it makes when tapped.

- -

⑪ Bottle Tune

1. Follow the pattern your teacher shows you to make a tune.

2. Now make up your own tune using the different bottles.

3. In the circles below, write the number of each bottle you tap to make your tune. Put them in order from left to right.

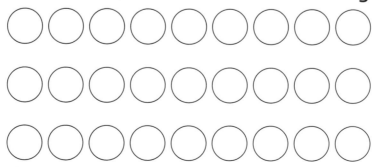

4. See if a friend can use the pattern to re-create your tune.

Sun and Shadows

Materials

- lab book pages 32–37, reproduced and fashioned into a booklet, one per student
- page 31, reproduced as an overhead transparency
- opaque objects, assorted shapes and sizes
- drinking glasses
- lamps or flashlights
- chalk
- clock
- clay
- stick or dowel

Objectives

- recall experiences with shadows
- identify the circumstances necessary for shadows to form
- demonstrate how long and short shadows are made
- recognize that opaque objects cast shadows while transparent objects do not
- track the movement of a shadow over time
- experiment with a simple sundial clock

Preparation

Find a cleared area outside where students can observe their own shadows, as well as shadows cast by other objects.

Gather a number of lamps or flashlights that students can use to make shadows in the classroom. Also collect a variety of opaque objects that students can use to try to create shadows. Choose objects of various sizes.

You will need to create a sundial with the class. To do so, place a stick or dowel into a piece of clay and stand it up in an open section of the schoolyard.

Background Information

Most students can tell you about the shadows that seem to follow them around wherever they go, but few may be able to explain how shadows are formed. They may know that the sun is involved, but not the exact position of objects needed to produce a shadow.

Shadows are created when light rays from the sun or another light source are blocked by an opaque object (an object that does not allow light to pass through it). In order for a shadow to be formed, the object must be in the path of the light rays and not, for example, within the shadow of a larger object. The light rays that are not blocked by the object illuminate the area beyond the object. The area directly behind the opaque object, on the other hand, remains dark as no light rays pass through the object to illuminate it. A shadow is always cast opposite from the light source that created it.

Sun and Shadows

Opaque objects do not let any light through, and therefore cast dark shadows. Translucent objects let some light through, and so cast light shadows. Transparent objects allow all light to pass through them, and therefore are incapable of casting shadows.

Objects on the ground outside create shadows as they block some of the sun's rays. As the sun moves across the sky over the course of the day, the positions of shadows change. (Of course, the sun only appears to move across the sky. It is the rotation of the Earth that causes this apparent motion to an observer on Earth.) A shadow cast to the west in the morning will be cast to the east in the evening. Shadows are longer in the morning and evening because the angle between the sun and the object is smaller. When the sun is directly above an object, it will cast no shadow at all.

Because the sun creates shadows on the ground, and the sun's position in the sky is related to the time of day, people have been using shadows to track time. While students cannot build a time-accurate sun clock, they can see how the changing position of shadows relates to the changing position of the sun and the time of day.

Assessment Ideas

Draw pictures of the sun and objects on the board in different relative positions and ask students to predict where the shadows would fall. Students should understand that a shadow always falls opposite the light source.

Extension Ideas

Have students cut out simple shapes of animals and other characters and use them to perform a shadow play for the class. Have them use their understanding of shadow-object-light positioning to set up the stage, puppets, and lights.

29

Page 1: Students may remember being outside on a sunny day and seeing their shadow on the ground. They may recall that it followed them as they moved.

Page 2: Direct students to draw their scenes as if they were looking at themselves from a distance. The picture should show the sun and shadow on opposite sides of the student.

Page 3: Again, drawings should show shadows and sun on opposite sides of the objects.

Page 4: 2) an object, a light source (sun) 3) either the second or third choices may be correct. Choice 1 is not correct.

Page 5: Pictures should show shadows and light source on either side of the object.

Page 6: 1) Long shadows are created by holding the light at a low angle to the object (i.e., low and to the side). 2) Short shadows are made by holding the light at close to a 90-degree angle to the object (i.e., right above it).

Page 7: Students will be able to make a shadow using a book, but will not be able to using the glass (or they will only be able to make a very faint shadow). When light is blocked by an object, a shadow is formed on the opposite side. When light is allowed to pass through an object, no shadow is formed. A drinking glass is transparent, meaning it lets light through. It cannot, therefore, form a shadow.

Page 8: 4) The shadow has changed position and maybe length.

Page 9: The picture should show three shadow positions, progressively moving in one direction.

Page 10: 1) As the sun moved across the sky, the shadow it cast also moved. 2) Answers will vary. 3) Answers will vary, but should be the opposite of #2. 4) The sun's position and my shadow's position are opposite.

Page 11: 3) Students might understand the connection between tracking shadows and tracking the movement of the sun and therefore the time of day. Make an overhead transparency of the picture on page 31. Explain how a real sundial works.

A Sundial

My Lab Book

Sun and Shadows

Name _____ Date _____

- -

1
Shadows All Around

Have you ever seen your shadow? Where were you when you saw it? What did it look like? Draw and describe what you remember.

Go outside. Stand in a place where you can see your shadow. Draw a picture that shows you, your shadow, and the position of the sun up in the sky.

- -

③
Other Shadows

Go outside again. Look for other shadows. What objects are making the shadows? Draw one of the objects, the shadow it makes, and the position of the sun.

④ Shadow Recipe

1. Look again at the drawings you made on pages 2 and 3 of your lab book.

2. What do you need to make a shadow?

   _____

   _____

3. Circle the choice that shows the correct order of the objects in your pictures.

   object-sun-shadow   shadow-object-sun   sun-object-shadow

- -

⑤ Making Shadows

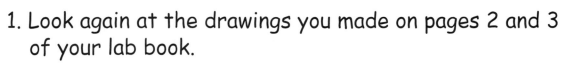

1. Use a lamp (or flashlight) and different objects to make as many different shadows as you can. Which one was your favorite?

2. Draw a picture to show how you created your favorite shadow. Where was the light? Where was the object? Where was the shadow?

❻ Long and Short

1. Pick one object. Use the lamp (or flashlight) to make the longest shadow you can using the object. How did you do it?

_____

_____

_____

2. Now use the lamp to create the shortest shadow you can. How did you do it?

_____

_____

_____

- -

❼ Block or Pass?

1. Try to make a shadow using a lamp (or flashlight) and a book. Could you do it?

_____

2. Try to make a shadow using a lamp and a drinking glass. Could you do it?

_____

3. Why do you think you could make a shadow with one object but not the other?

_____

_____

❽ Changing Shadow

1. Go outside in the morning. Choose a partner to work with. Stand in a spot on the hard playground where you cast a shadow.

2. Have your partner trace around your feet and your shadow. Then have your partner stand while you trace his or her feet and shadow. Notice where the sun is in the sky.

3. Come back to the same place at lunchtime. Stand in the same spot, right in the footmarks you made before. Have your partner trace your shadow again. Then trace your partner's shadow.

4. How has your shadow changed? How has the position of the sun changed?

_____

_____

- -

❾ More Changes

1. Go outside again in the afternoon. Stand in the same spot as before and have your partner trace your shadow. Then trace your partner's shadow.

2. Draw a picture that shows what your shadow looked like this morning, at lunchtime, and this afternoon. Also draw the position of the sun.

⑩ Shadow Behavior

1. Why do you think your shadow moved from morning to afternoon?

   _____

   _____

2. Which way did the sun move during the day? From right to left, or left to right?

   _____

3. Which way did your shadow move?

   _____

4. How is the sun's position related to your shadow's position?

   _____

- -

⑪ Shadow Clock

1. Go outside. Look at the shadow clock your teacher set up. On the picture below, draw where the stick's shadow is. Then draw where you think the shadow will be at the end of the school day.

2. Go back and look at the clock when school is over for the day. Draw where the stick shadow is.

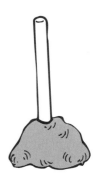

3. How could you use shadows to tell the time of day?

   _____

   _____

Nutrition

Materials

- lab book pages 42–47, reproduced and fashioned into a booklet, one per student
- page 41, reproduced as an overhead transparency
- packaged foods, assorted (crackers, condiments, canned fruits and vegetables)
- brown paper grocery bags
- vegetable oil
- water
- paper towels
- trays
- fresh foods, assorted (fruits, vegetables)
- fruit and vegetable juices, assorted (apple, grape, orange, tomato, carrot)
- cornstarch
- gallon container
- iodine
- glass jars, small
- droppers
- dishes, small
- chicken bones
- vinegar
- large glass jar, with lid

Objectives

- give examples of healthy and unhealthy foods
- identify the ingredients in a packaged food
- conduct fat, Vitamin C, and starch tests on various foods
- recognize the importance of calcium for strong bones
- plan a healthy meal based on the Food Guide Pyramid

Preparation

Two weeks before starting the unit, place a number of small, cooked chicken bones (meat removed) in a large glass jar. Fill the jar with vinegar and put the lid on the jar. Let the jar sit for two weeks, then pull out the bones and set them on paper towels to dry thoroughly. Thoroughly clean another bunch of cooked chicken bones.

Note: Before you begin the unit, remind students that they are working in a science lab, and that they are not to eat anything in a science lab unless told to do so by you.

Collect a variety of different packaged foods. Make sure the packages have a nutrition facts panel, and that there are not too many total ingredients or hard-to-pronounce words. Students will read the labels and write the ingredients in their lab books.

Prepare trays of assorted food pieces for students to conduct their fat and starch tests on. Cut up small pieces of fresh fruit and vegetables, as well as pieces of processed starchy foods like crackers and cookies.

Collect an assortment of juices for students to test for Vitamin C content. Decide how you will distribute the juices to students. Each group will need one small glass jar and one dropper for each juice tested.

Make the Vitamin C indicator liquid (one gallon) by mixing a heaping teaspoon of cornstarch in a cup of cold water. Boil this mixture for two minutes. Put ten droppers full of this mixture into a gallon container of water. Add one dropper full of iodine. Cap the container and shake until mixture looks uniformly blue.

38

Background Information

An understanding of the nutritional value of different food is essential for lifelong health. Many students are not aware of the nutritional value of the foods they eat every day. Most students eat more fat and sugar than recommended by the USDA's Food Guide Pyramid.

Processed foods are often the worst nutritional offenders. In order to keep foods from spoiling on the shelves of supermarkets, preservatives and other chemicals are added. Oftentimes, these chemicals and other additives are not particularly good for you.

A chicken bone soaked for a period of time in vinegar will be depleted of its calcium. (The calcium will crystallize out in the vinegar solution. You'll be able to see the crystals.) A bone without calcium is much weaker than a bone with calcium. Hence the soaked bone is bendable when wet and brittle once dried.

The USDA Food Guide Pyramid was developed to help people make healthy food choices. It shows the recommended amounts of different food types that people should be consuming daily. Carbohydrates make up the base of the pyramid (the greatest number of servings), while fats and sweets make up the top (the least number of servings).

Assessment Ideas

Have students create a list of foods they want to start eating more of, and a list of foods they would like to eat less of. Have them explain what it is about each food that makes it a good or bad choice for their diet.

Extension Ideas

Have students research the role of carbohydrates, fats, and protein in their diets. Which types of nutrients are especially needed by athletes? by children? by teenagers? How do a person's nutritional needs change throughout his or her lifetime?

39

Lab Book Instructions & Answers

Page 1: Discuss student responses as a class.

Page 2: Distribute packaged foods to each student or group. Help students as needed with ingredients they have never heard of.

Page 3: Distribute a piece of brown paper, water, and vegetable oil to each student or group. Arrange class time for the papers to dry. 3) Both liquids left a wet spot. 4) Only the oil spot is still there. Explain that foods with fat leave a mark that does not dry on the paper.

Page 4: Distribute trays of assorted foods (see "Preparation"). 2) Foods high in fat include processed snack foods like crackers and cookies, as well as some vegetables, like avocados. 3) Answers will vary.

Page 5: Students wil need glass jars and Vitamin C indicator liquid. 3) Each is a slightly different color.

Page 6: 2) Answers will vary, but orange juice contains a lot of Vitamin C. 3) Answers will vary according to the juices tested.

Page 7: Distribute potato slices, dishes, and iodine to students. Warn them to be careful when using the iodine and not to get it near their eyes or mouth, or on their clothes. 3) dark brown or black; 4) yes; 5) Answers will vary.

Page 8: 2) Answers will vary according to foods tested.

Page 9: Label the bones soaked in vinegar "A" and the unsoaked bones "B." Give each student or group one of each. 4) Calcium makes bones strong.

Page 10: Make an overhead transparency of the Food Guide Pyramid on page 41.

Page 11: Show the Food Guide Pyramid again on the overhead projector.

40

Food Guide Pyramid

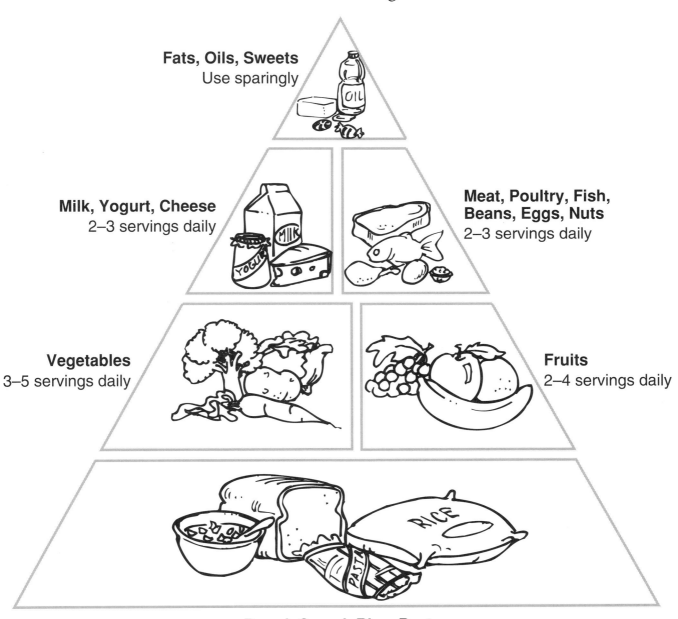

Fats, Oils, Sweets
Use sparingly

Milk, Yogurt, Cheese
2–3 servings daily

Meat, Poultry, Fish, Beans, Eggs, Nuts
2–3 servings daily

Vegetables
3–5 servings daily

Fruits
2–4 servings daily

Bread, Cereal, Rice, Pasta
6–11 servings daily

My Lab Book

Nutrition

Name _____   Date _____

---

❶
Favorite Foods

1. What are some of your favorite foods? Think about things you eat for breakfast, lunch, snacks, and dinner.

_____

_____

_____

_____

_____

2. Circle the foods you think are healthy. Underline the foods you think are unhealthy, or "junk food."

② What's Inside?

1. Look at the food package your teacher gives you. Write down all the ingredients you think are inside the food.

_____

_____

_____

2. Now read the label on the side of the package. Write down all the ingredients listed. Circle the ingredients you don't know.

_____

_____

_____

_____

- -

③ Fat Test (1)

1. Spread a drop of water on a piece of brown paper.

2. Spread a drop of oil a few inches away from the waterdrop.

3. Hold the paper up to the light. Describe the mark left by both drops.

_____

_____

4. Let the paper dry for an hour. Describe what the marks look like now.

_____

_____

Fat Test (2)
④

1. Look at the foods your teacher gives you. Which do you think have fat in them? Record your predictions on the chart.

2. Use the brown paper to test the foods for fat. Record your results on the chart.

Food	Prediction: Has Fat?	Result: Has Fat?

3. Circle the food that seemed to have the most fat.

- -

Vitamin C Test (1)
⑤

You can use a chemical to test how much Vitamin C is in different kinds of juice. Follow these directions to do the test:

1. Pour 2 tablespoons of the blue liquid into each jar. Set the jars on a piece of white paper.

2. Add 10 drops of juice to each jar. Swirl the liquid in the jar.

3. What do you notice about the jars?

_____

_____

4. Line up the jars in order from lightest blue to darkest blue.

⑥ Vitamin C Test (2)

1. The jar with the lightest blue color contains the most Vitamin C. The jar with the darkest blue color contains the least Vitamin C.

2. Which jar is the lightest color? Which juice contains the most Vitamin C?

_____

3. List the juices you tested in order from Most Vitamin C to Least Vitamin C.

Most Vitamin C					Least Vitamin C

- -

⑦ Starch Test (1)

1. Iodine is a chemical you can use to test for starch in foods. Our bodies use starch for energy.

2. Put a piece of potato in a dish.

3. Place a few drops of iodine on the potato. What color does the iodine turn? _____

4. If the iodine turns purple, dark brown, or black, the potato contains starch. Does the potato contain starch?_____

5. List some foods that you think contain a lot of starch.

_____

Starch Test (2)

8

1. Use iodine to give different foods the starch test.

2. Record your results on the chart.

Food Tested	Iodine Color	Does It Contain Starch?

- -

Strong Bones

9

1. Look at the two chicken bones your teacher gives you.

2. Snap each bone in half. Which one breaks more easily?

_____

3. Bone A has been soaked in vinegar to remove the calcium inside the bone. Bone B has not been soaked in vinegar.

4. Why do you think it's important to have enough calcium in the foods you eat?

_____

_____

⑩ Food Pyramid

1. Look at the Food Guide Pyramid on the overhead projector.

2. Plan one healthy day of eating based on the information you see in the pyramid.

Breakfast: _____

_____

Lunch: _____

_____

Dinner: _____

_____

- -

⑪ How Healthy?

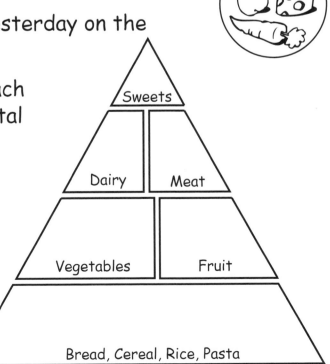

1. Write down everything you ate yesterday on the back of this page.

2. About how many servings from each group did you have? Write the total numbers on the chart.

3. Did you have a healthy day yesterday?

_____

_____

_____

Cold and Heat

Materials

- lab book pages 52–57, reproduced and fashioned into a booklet, one per student
- page 51, reproduced as an overhead transparency
- bowls, plastic
- warm water
- cold water
- thermometers (with °C and °F scales)
- erasable marker, red
- cups, plastic
- ice, cubed and crushed
- stopwatch or clock
- shredded newspaper or other insulation
- jars, glass
- black construction paper
- white construction paper
- tape

Objectives

- observe that skin can only feel differences in temperature
- recognize that heat moves from hotter objects to colder objects
- use a thermometer to measure temperature
- experiment with variables that affect ice cube melting time
- compare the absorption of solar energy by white and black surfaces

Preparation

Gather enough thermometers so that each student or group has one to work with. The thermometers should show Celsius as well as Fahrenheit scales.

Collect crushed ice and cubed ice for students to use in their experiments. You may want to keep the bags of ice in a cooler in the classroom on days they are needed.

Gather some insulative materials, such as shredded newspaper, old rags, packing peanuts, and so on. Students will be given the opportunity to use the materials when designing a way to keep their ice cubes from melting.

Students will need to time how long it takes for their ice cubes to melt. Make sure the class clock has a second hand and that students know how to tell time. Otherwise, provide stopwatches, or keep track of the time together as a class.

Locate a place outside where your class can set their glass jars for several hours. The spot should be sunny the whole time, and be safe from anyone who might want to tamper with the experiment.

Background Information

What we call "heat," most scientists call "thermal energy." Heat is a form of energy, and like all energy, it can be transferred from one object or place to another.

The laws of thermodynamics say that heat always moves from warmer areas to colder areas. Thus heat will never move from a 50°F object to a 70°F object it is in contact with. Nor will it move from a 60°F room to a 80°F room.

Human skin cannot sense absolute temperatures. It can only sense relative temperatures. Thus a hand soaking in cold water will feel warm when placed in a bowl of lukewarm water, while a hand soaking in hot water will feel cold when moved to the same bowl.

Most Americans use the Fahrenheit scale to measure temperature. Scientists prefer the Celsius scale. Because most weather services use the Fahrenheit scale, it is useful for students to be familiar with it. But they should be making most of their scientific measurements using the Celsius scale.

Several variables affect the rate at which an ice cube will melt (change from a solid to a liquid state). One variable is cube size. Larger cubes have a lower surface area-to-volume ratio, and so will be exposed to less warm air and will therefore melt more slowly than smaller cubes. This is why crushed ice melts faster than whole cubes. Two equal-sized cubes placed in cold and warm water baths will melt at different rates. The warmer bath will transfer more thermal energy to the cube, thus melting it faster. Insulative materials, such as shredded newspaper, will prevent the exchange of thermal energy between a cube and the air around it, thus slowing the rate at which the cube melts.

Dark surfaces absorb more energy from the sun than lighter surfaces. For example, a jar of water wrapped in black paper will get warmer than the same amount of water wrapped in white paper.

Assessment Ideas

Review with students the fact that heat moves from warmer objects to colder objects. Have them use this information to explain what happened in their ice cube melting experiments. (In each case, heat energy was transferred from the warmer environment to the ice cube, eventually melting it.)

Extension Ideas

Have students do more experiments with solar energy. Do large amounts of water heat up more quickly or more slowly than smaller amounts in the same size container? Does the same amount of water heat up more quickly in a deep or a shallow container?

Page 1: Each student or group will need one bowl of warm water, one bowl of cold water, and one bowl of room-temperature water. 4) Students should realize that their hands felt relative warmth or coolness, depending on the temperature of their hands going in.

Page 2: hand to snowball; warm water to cold air; warm forehead to cold washcloth; warm soda to ice cube.

Page 3: Make an overhead transparency of the thermometer on page 51. Use an erasable marking pen to show three different Celsius temperatures on the thermometer scale. Each student or group will need a thermometer and a cup of water.

Page 4: Distribute a cup full of ice and a cup of crushed ice to each student or group. 2) The whole cubes are larger than the crushed ones. 4) the one with the crushed ice; 5) Smaller cubes are exposed to more warm air and so melt faster.

Page 5: Each student or group will need one cup of warm water, one cup of cold water, and two equal-sized ice cubes. 3) the one in the warm water; 4) The water surrounding the cube was warmer and so it melted the cube faster. You may want to discuss the transfer of energy here with students.

Page 6: Cold water baths/large cubes are two variables that slow down melt time.

Page 7: If they haven't already used them, present the insulative materials.

Page 8: Warm water baths and small cubes are two variables that speed up melt time.

Page 9: Students might suggest placing their cubes in a warm water bath out in the sun.

Page 10: Prepare the jars for students, or have them wrap the jars in black and white construction paper themselves.

Page 11: Help students as needed with the subtraction problem. 4) the black jar; 5) black.

50

See page 50 "Page 3" for instructions on how to use the art on this page.

Thermometer

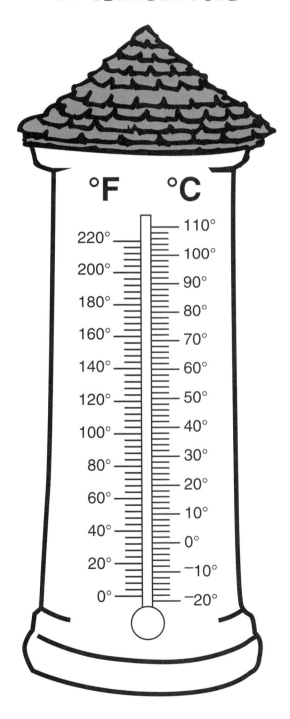

51

My Lab Book
Cold and Heat

Name _____   Date _____

- -

❶
Water Bath

1. Put your left hand in a bowl of warm water. Put your right hand in a bowl of cold water. Leave them there for about a minute.

2. Take your left hand out of the warm water and put it in the third bowl of water. How does the water feel?_____

3. Take your right hand out of the cold water and put it in the third bowl of water. How does the water feel?_____

4. Why do you think each hand felt different in the third bowl?

_____

_____

❷ Heat Moves

1. Heat is a kind of energy. It only moves from hotter things to colder things. It cannot move from colder things to hotter things.

2. Draw an arrow to show how heat moves between each of the following pairs of objects.

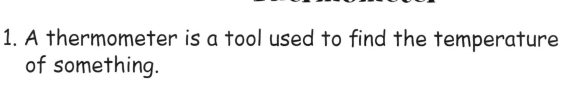

snowball	your hand
warm ocean water	cold air above water
cold washcloth	forehead of person with a fever
ice cube	warm soda

---

❸ Thermometer

1. A thermometer is a tool used to find the temperature of something.

2. Look at the overhead of the thermometer. Your teacher will show three different temperatures on the thermometer. Write them below. Remember to write the units (°C).

_____   _____   _____

3. Use the thermometer to take the temperature of a cup of water. Stick the bulb end of the thermometer in the cup and let it sit at least one minute. Then read the temperature on the scale.

4. What is the temperature? _____

❹ Cube Size and Melting Time

1. Look at the cup of crushed ice. Now look at the cup of whole ice.

2. Compare the size of the ice pieces in each cup.

   _____

3. Which cup of ice do you think will melt first? Why?

   _____

4. Let the cups of ice melt. Which melted first? _____

5. Why do you think one cup of ice melted faster than the other?

   _____

   _____

- -

❺ Bath Temperature and Melting Time

1. Use the thermometers to find the temperature of the water in each cup. Record the temperatures below, including units.

   Cup 1: _____ Cup 2: _____

2. Place an ice cube in each cup. Which ice cube do you think will melt first? Why?

   _____

3. Let the ice cubes melt. Which melted first? _____

4. Why do you think one ice cube melted faster than the other?

   _____

❻
Stay Frozen! (1)

1. How do you think you can make an ice cube in a cup on your desk stay frozen as long as possible? Look back at pages 4 and 5 to see what kinds of things affected how fast the ice cubes melted. Then write your ideas below.

_____

_____

_____

_____

_____

2. Test out your idea. Time how long it takes for your ice cube to melt.

   Melting Time: _____ min _____ sec

- -

❼
Stay Frozen! (2)

1. How could you improve your design to make the cube stay frozen even longer?

_____

_____

_____

2. Try out your new design. Then time how long it takes for your new ice cube to melt.

   Melting Time: _____ min _____ sec

3. Did the second cube stay frozen longer?

_____

Melt! **8** (1)

1. How do you think you can make an ice cube in a cup on your desk melt as quickly as possible? Look back at pages 4 and 5 to see what kinds of things affected how fast the ice cubes melted. Then write your ideas below.

_____

_____

_____

_____

_____

2. Test out your idea. Time how long it takes for your ice cube to melt.

Melting Time: _____ min _____ sec

- -

Melt! **9** (2)

1. How could you improve your design to make the cube melt even faster?

_____

_____

_____

2. Try out your new design. Then time how long it takes for your new ice cube to melt.

Melting Time: _____ min _____ sec

3. Did the second cube melt faster?

_____

Absorbing Energy (1)

1. Take the temperature of the water in each jar. Record the temperatures in the Start Temp column of the chart below.

Jar	Start Temp (°C)	Finish Temp (°C)	Temp Change (°C)
Black Paper			
White Paper			

2. You are going to place both jars outside in the sun for several hours. Which jar do you think will heat up the most? Why?

_____

_____

- -

Absorbing Energy (2)

1. Place both jars outside in the sun for several hours.

2. Take the temperature of the water in both jars. Record the temperatures in the Finish Temp column of the chart on page 10.

3. Subtract the number in the Start Temp column from the number in the Finish Temp column. This tells you how much the temperature changed in each jar.

4. Which jar had the greater increase in temperature? _____

5. Which color is better at absorbing the sun's energy, white or black? _____

Air

Materials

- lab book pages 62–67, reproduced and fashioned into a booklet, one per student
- page 61, reproduced as an overhead transparency
- balloons, medium-sized, identical
- jars, glass
- cold water
- hot water
- soil, gardening
- string
- yardstick
- tacks
- paper towels
- cups, clear plastic
- tubs, plastic
- bags, plastic, resealable
- books
- bottles, plastic
- talcum powder
- lamp with exposed bulb
- washers, aluminum
- plastic sheets, 30-cm square
- tape

Objectives

- demonstrate that air is a substance that takes up space and has weight
- observe that air can be found in water and soil
- demonstrate that air volume increases with temperature
- observe that hot air rises
- demonstrate the usefulness of air resistance for slowing the rate at which objects fall
- use the Beaufort Wind Speed Scale to estimate wind speed

Preparation

Collect some gardening soil. Make sure it does not have too high of a clay content. Rich, organic soils work best. Locate a sunny windowsill or spot outside where students can leave jars of water for a few hours.

You will need a lamp with the shade removed to demonstrate how warm air above the bulb rises. Use an extension cord as needed to place the lamp where all students can see it.

Cut 30-cm-square sheets of plastic from green garbage bags to act as parachutes. Cut several 30-cm lengths of string to attach the parachutes to the washers.

Locate a spot outdoors where you can have students measure the wind speed using the Beaufort Wind Speed Scale. The area should be as open as possible.

Background Information

Many students think that because they can't see air, it doesn't exist. Activities at the beginning of this unit demonstrate that air takes up space and has weight.

Air is everywhere, not just floating around us. It is dissolved in water and located between solid materials that make up soil. Air can be seen under water when it forms visible bubbles.

As the temperature of any gas rises, so does the volume of space it takes up (unless that space is not expandable). Thus, when air in a balloon is heated, the air expands and the balloon inflates more.

Hot air rises. The air directly above a hot light bulb will create an upward current. Particles light enough to be carried by the draft will float upward when sprinkled above the hot bulb.

Air molecules resist the downward movement of falling objects. Parachutes make use of this resistance to slow the rate at which objects fall to Earth. They do so by "capturing" as many air molecules as possible during their descent. This is why the canopy of a parachute is always wider than the falling object.

The Beaufort Wind Speed Scale was designed in the 1800s by Admiral Francis Beaufort of Britain. The scale allows people to estimate wind speed based on visible effects of the wind on objects around them.

Assessment Ideas

Draw a concept map on the board and have students fill in the terms that show their understanding of the properties of air they learned about in this unit.

Extension Ideas

Hold a parachute contest to see who can make a parachute that results in the slowest fall.

59

Lab Book Instructions & Answers

Page 1: Each student or group will need one balloon and a jar or cup of water. 2) air; 3) The balloon flies around. As the air escapes, it pushes the balloon in the opposite direction. 4) bubbles.

Page 2: Each student or group will need a jar, some cold water, and some soil. 3) soil, water, bubbles of air; 4) bubbles of air; 5) The air was in the soil.

Page 3: Each student or group will need a jar and some cold water. 2) water; 4) bubbles in the water; 5) The air was in the water and came out as bubbles when the water warmed.

Page 4: Tie a string in the center of a yardstick and suspend the stick from a doorway or other place. Each student or group will need two identical balloons, two pieces of string, and a tack. 4) the end with the inflated balloon dropped; 5) without the weight of the air in the popped balloon, the other side weighed more.

Page 5: Each student or group will need a paper towel, a plastic cup, and a tub of water. 5) No, the air made a pocket that protected the towel from the water.

Page 6: Each student will need one book and one resealable bag. 4) By filling the bag with air, I was able to make a sort of air pillow and lift the book off the table.

Page 7: Basketball: Air helps make the ball bouncy. Life vest: Air makes the vest float and keeps the person wearing it afloat. Foam packing peanuts: Air makes the peanuts light and fluffy so they can protect objects packed in them. Car air bag: Air makes a cushion so that the people don't hit the dash or windshield.

Page 8: Each student or group will need a balloon, a bottle, and a tub with hot water in it. 3) The balloon will inflate after a few minutes in the hot water bath.

Page 9: You may prefer to do this experiment as a class demonstration. 1) The powder falls over the lamp. 3) The powder rises up in a flume above the bulb. 4) The bulb warmed the air above it. Warm air rises. The powder is light enough to be carried up by this moving air.

Page 10: Each student or group will need a washer, a sheet of plastic, and four lengths of string. 1) It falls quickly to the ground. 2) air; 4) It fell more slowly.

Page 11: Make a copy of the Beaufort Wind Speed Scale on page 61 for each student. Take students outdoors and have them determine the wind speed.

60

Beaufort Wind Speed Scale

Symbol	Speed (kph)	Beaufort Scale Number	Description (What the Wind Does)
	less than 2	0	Calm; smoke goes straight up
	2–5	1	Light air; smoke blown by wind
	6–11	2	Light breeze; wind felt on face
	12–19	3	Gentle breeze; extends a light flag
	20–29	4	Moderate breeze; raises dust and loose paper
	30–38	5	Fresh breeze; small trees begin to sway
	39–50	6	Strong breeze; umbrellas become hard to use
	51–61	7	Moderate gale; difficult to walk
	62–74	8	Fresh gale; twigs broken off trees
	75–86	9	Strong gale; roof damage
	87–102	10	Whole gale; trees uprooted
	103–117	11	Storm winds; widespread damage
	118 and up	12	Hurricane; violent destruction

My Lab Book

Air

Name _____ Date _____

---

❶
What's Inside?

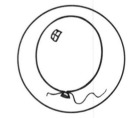

1. Blow up your balloon and pinch the end closed.

2. What is inside your balloon?

_____

3. Let go of the end of the balloon. What happens? Why?

_____

_____

4. Blow up your balloon again and pinch the end closed. Hold the end under water and then let it go. What do you see?

_____

❷ Soil Mystery

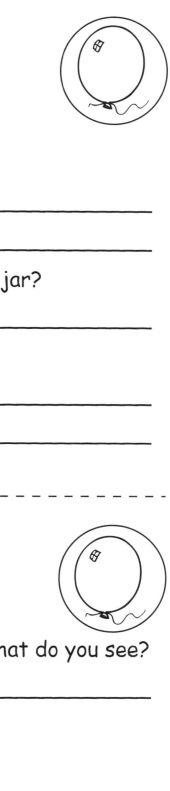

1. Fill the jar halfway with cold water.

2. Pour about a cup of soil into the jar.

3. Name all the things you see in the jar.

   _____

   _____

4. Do you see anything besides soil and water in the jar?

   _____

5. Where do you think these new things came from?

   _____

   _____

- -

❸ Water Mystery

1. Fill the jar with cold water.

2. Look at the water through the side of the jar. What do you see?

   _____

3. Place the jar in a sunny spot for a few hours.

4. Look at the water again. What do you see now?

   _____

   _____

5. Where do you think these new things came from?

   _____

❹ Balancing Act

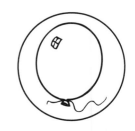

1. Blow up two balloons to the same size.

2. Use string to tie one balloon to each end of the yardstick your teacher has hung up.

3. When the stick is straight, that means the weight of the balloons on each end is equal.

4. Now pop one of the balloons. What happens to the stick?

_____

5. How can you explain what happened to the stick?

_____

_____

_____

- -

❺ Down Under

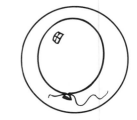

1. Crumple up a paper towel. Push it into the bottom of a cup.

2. Turn the cup upside down. Make sure the towel stays in the cup when you turn it over.

3. Lower the cup, upside down, into a tub of water. Hold it there for a few seconds.

4. Pull the cup straight up out of the water and remove the towel.

5. Is the paper towel wet? How can you explain what you see?

_____

_____

❻ Lift a Book

1. Look at the plastic bag and the book.

2. How can you use the bag to lift the book an inch off your desk? Write your ideas below.

   _____

   _____

   _____

3. Test out your idea. Did it work? _____

4. Explain how you used air to lift the book.

   _____

   _____

   _____

- -

❼ Air at Work

Here is a list of objects that contain air. Next to each one, write how the air helps the object do its job.

- basketball _____

  _____

- life vest _____

  _____

- foam packing peanuts _____

  _____

- car air bags _____

  _____

❽ Air and Temperature

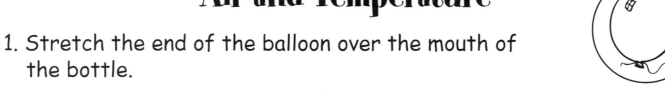

1. Stretch the end of the balloon over the mouth of the bottle.

2. Draw what the balloon looks like in the box on the left.

Before Hot Water Bath	In Hot Water Bath

3. Now place the bottle in a hot water bath. Let it sit for several minutes. Then draw what the balloon looks like again.

- -

❾ Hot Air

1. Sprinkle some talcum powder over the bulb of an unplugged lamp. Describe what happens to the powder.

_____

2. Now plug in the lamp. Wait a few minutes.

3. Sprinkle the powder again over the light bulb. Describe what happens to the powder this time.

_____

4. How can you explain what happened to the powder?

_____

_____

Hands-On Science • EMC 5000 • ©2003 by Evan-Moor Corp.

⑩
Look Out Below

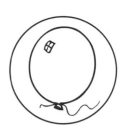

1. Hold your arm out and drop the washer. Describe how it falls.

_____

_____

2. What did the washer fall through on its way to the ground?

_____

3. Tape a piece of string to each corner of the plastic sheet. Tie the strings to the washer to make a parachute.

4. Drop the washer like you did before. Describe how it falls.

_____

_____

- -

⑪
Blowing in the Wind

1. What is wind? _____

_____

2. Some days, the wind blows strong. Other days, it does not.

3. Look at the Beaufort Wind Speed Scale your teacher gives you.

4. Go outside. Use the pictures to determine how windy it is today on the Beaufort Scale, and in kilometers per hour.

Description of Wind	Beaufort Scale Number	Speed (kph)

Bubbles

Materials

- lab book pages 72–77, reproduced and fashioned into a booklet, one per student

- page 71, reproduced as an overhead transparency

- dishwashing liquid

- glycerin

- water

- pail

- wooden spoon

- plastic cups, clear

- paper towels

- pipe cleaners

- stopwatch or clock with second hand

- dishes, shallow

- straws, drinking

- thread or thin string

- scissors

- cookie sheets

Objectives

- compare plain water to bubble solution

- experiment with wand shape and bubble shape

- conclude that all (single) bubbles are round, regardless of wand shape

- observe interactions between bubbles

- recognize the colors of light on the surface of bubbles

- use language skills in creating a story about an imaginary bubble ride

Preparation

Prepare a large pail of bubble solution for the class to use in their experiments. In a pail, mix 2 parts dishwashing liquid with 1 part glycerin and 6 parts water. Experiment with the solution, adding more glycerin (to make the bubbles grow bigger and last longer) as needed.

Collect pipe cleaners or wires for students to use in making their wands. The wire should be flexible enough for students to bend easily. Also, it should have no sharp ends that might cause injury.

As bubbles fall on the classroom floor and burst, a slippery film can build up, causing a safety hazard. Consider conducting the bubble-blowing activities outside, or in a carpeted area of the school.

Warn students that bubble solution is soapy water, and it can irritate their eyes. Advise them not to rub their eyes when working with the bubble solution. Keep plenty of paper towels handy for students to wipe off their hands. They should also avoid blowing bubbles directly into each other's faces.

Students will need to time how long it takes for their bubbles to burst. If you don't have a clock with a second hand in the classroom, hand out stopwatches, or count off the time yourself.

Locate a place outside where students can blow their bubbles and see how sunlight creates a rainbow on the surface of the bubbles. The area should get direct sunlight.

Prepare a bubble frame for each student or group as follows: Cut a straw in half. Run about 1 to 2 feet of thread or thin string through both straws and tie off the string in a knot. Pull the knot into one of the straws.

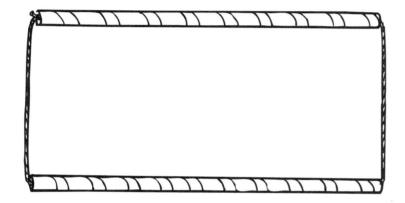

Background Information

A bubble is a quantity of air trapped inside a thin skin of liquid (soapy water). Soap makes water more elastic so that it can stretch better. Glycerin reduces the rate at which water on the bubble's surface evaporates. When the water evaporates, the bubble dries out and bursts.

Bubbles are always round, regardless of the wand shape that created them. That's because the soapy water that forms the bubble tries to pull itself into the smallest shape possible once it leaves the wand, and the smallest shape possible is a sphere.

Assessment Ideas

Ask students to explain how bubbles are formed and how they behave.

Extension Ideas

Have students research bubble tricks, including making a "square" bubble inside of another bubble.

69

Page 1: Each student or group will need one cup of plain water and one cup of bubble solution. Supply paper towels for cleanup. 3) The bubble mix feels slippery; the plain water does not. 4) Students may guess that slippery water makes the best bubbles because bubbles are slippery, too.

Page 2: Each student will need one pipe cleaner or wire. Help students as needed to form a wand with a round loop on the end and a long handle.

Page 3: Each student or group will need a cup of bubble solution and their wands. 4) When they touch the floor, or a person or other object, or sometimes just after a while, they will pop. Explain that when bubbles dry out, they pop. They need to stay wet to stay "alive."

Page 4: Each team of two will need one cup of bubble solution and their wands. 4) They either joined together or bounced off each other. The more gently the bubbles are blown, the more likely they are to join together.

Page 5: Each team of two will need one cup of bubble solution and their wands. 3) The bubble popped. 5) probably; 6) The bubble mix made a film on my hand that kept the bubble wet so it didn't pop.

Page 6: Each student or group will need a dish, some bubble mix, and a straw. 5) by dipping the straw into the mix again while it was still in the first bubble, and blowing another bubble.

Page 7: Make an overhead transparency of the first picture on page 71. Each student will need one pipe cleaner and a cup of bubble solution. 1) round; 5) round; 6) No, they are all round.

Page 8: Take students outside to a sunny area. Each student or group will need one cup of bubble solution and their wands. 4) colors of the rainbow; 5) the colors twirl and move. Explain that as sunlight passes through the surface of the bubbles, it is bent and shows all its different colors—the colors of the rainbow.

Page 9: Pass out the bubble frames to students. They will also need some bubble solution poured into a cookie sheet. Provide paper towels for cleanup. 2) colors of the rainbow; 3) The hand must be coated in bubble solution in order to pass through the frame without breaking the film.

Page 10: Encourage students to think about their ideas before drawing their pictures. They should have the story in their heads before they draw it.

Page 11: Student stories should describe the scene they drew on page 10.

See page 70 "Page 7" for instructions on how to use the art on this page.

Wacky Wands

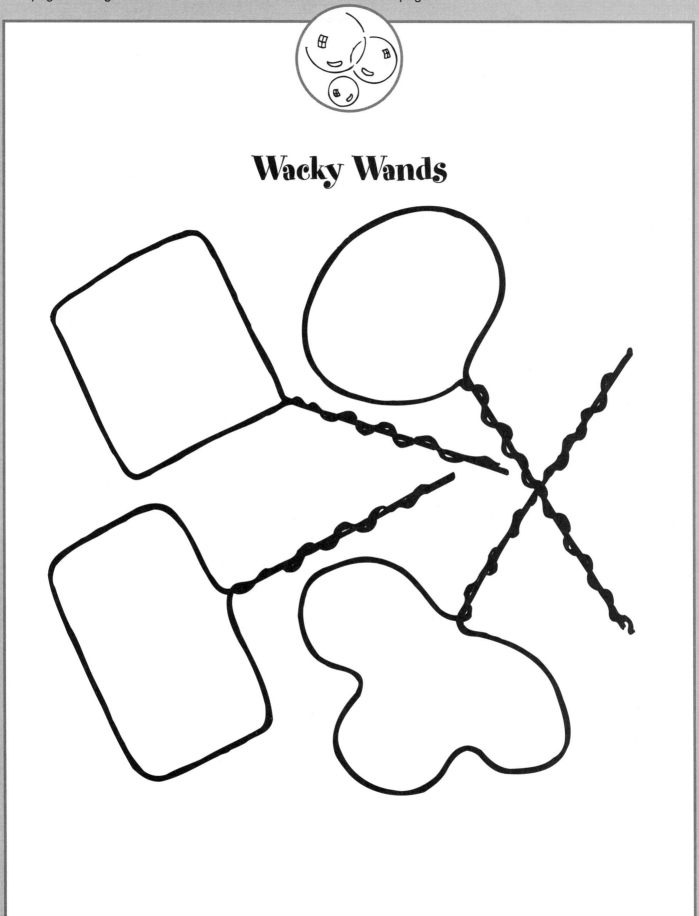

71

My Lab Book
Bubbles

Name _____ Date _____

- -

❶
Bubble Bath

1. Stick the fingers of one hand in the cup of plain water. Rub your fingers together.

2. Stick the fingers of your other hand in the cup of bubble mix. Rub your fingers together.

3. What difference do you feel?

_____

_____

4. Why do you think bubble mix feels the way it does?

_____

❷ Bubble Wand

1. Before you can make bubbles, you need to make a bubble wand.

2. Bend the top of a pipe cleaner to make a loop at the end. Twist the end around the handle.

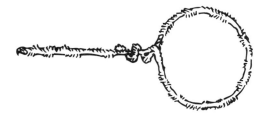

3. What shape do you think the bubbles you make with this wand will be?

_____

- -

❸ Bubble Fun

1. Dip your wand in the bubble mix. Blow some bubbles.

2. Blow the biggest bubble you can.

3. Now blow the smallest bubble you can.

4. When do bubbles break? What makes them break?

_____

_____

5. Time how many seconds you can make a bubble last.

_____ seconds

④ Bubble Buddy

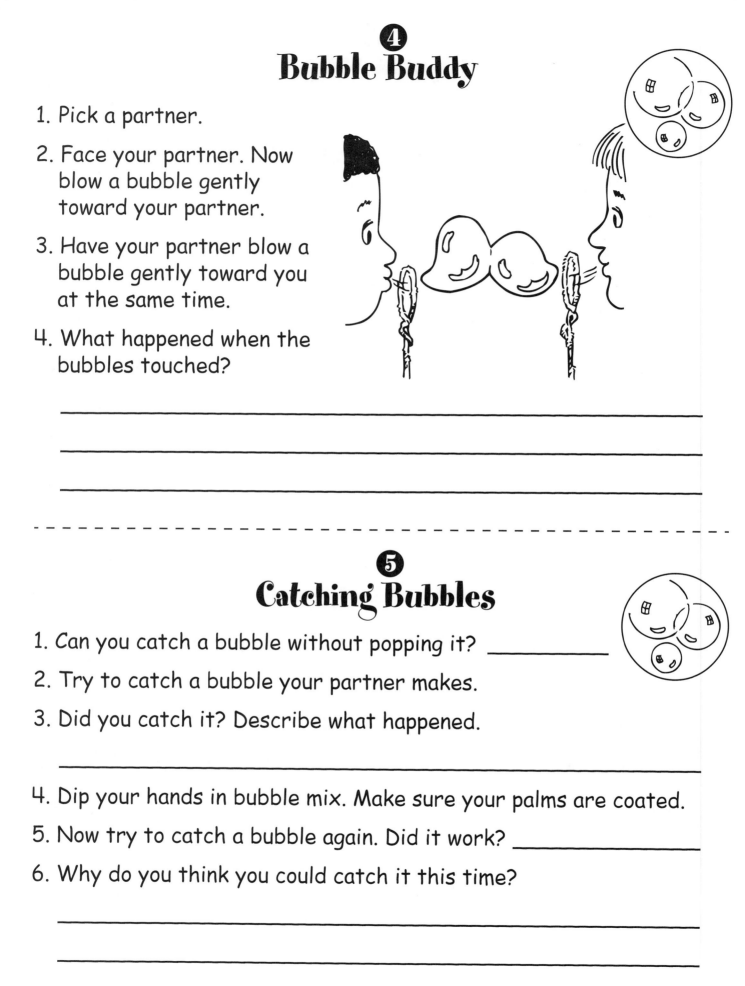

1. Pick a partner.

2. Face your partner. Now blow a bubble gently toward your partner.

3. Have your partner blow a bubble gently toward you at the same time.

4. What happened when the bubbles touched?

_____

_____

_____

- -

⑤ Catching Bubbles

1. Can you catch a bubble without popping it? _____

2. Try to catch a bubble your partner makes.

3. Did you catch it? Describe what happened.

_____

4. Dip your hands in bubble mix. Make sure your palms are coated.

5. Now try to catch a bubble again. Did it work? _____

6. Why do you think you could catch it this time?

_____

_____

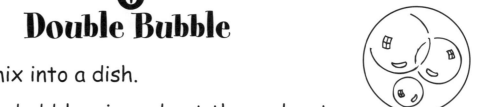

⑥ Double Bubble

1. Pour some bubble mix into a dish.

2. Dip a straw into the bubble mix and get the end wet.

3. Hold the straw end just above the dish and blow until you make a bubble on the dish.

4. Can you blow another bubble inside this bubble? Try out your ideas.

5. How were you able to blow another bubble inside the first bubble?

_____

_____

_____

_____

- -

⑦ Wacky Wands

1. What shape are bubbles? _____

2. How could you make a square bubble? Write down your ideas.

_____

3. Look at the wand shapes on the overhead projector. Use a new pipe cleaner to make one of the shapes.

4. Dip your "wacky wand" in bubble mix and blow a bubble.

5. What shape is the bubble? _____

6. Try it again. Could you make a bubble that was the same shape as the wand? _____

➑ Bubble Rainbow

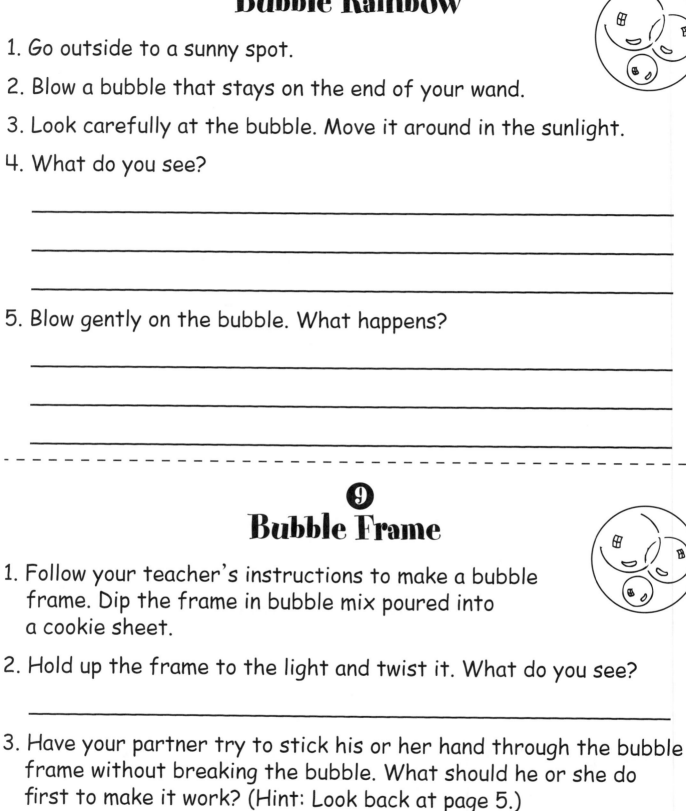

1. Go outside to a sunny spot.

2. Blow a bubble that stays on the end of your wand.

3. Look carefully at the bubble. Move it around in the sunlight.

4. What do you see?

_____

_____

_____

5. Blow gently on the bubble. What happens?

_____

_____

_____

- -

➒ Bubble Frame

1. Follow your teacher's instructions to make a bubble frame. Dip the frame in bubble mix poured into a cookie sheet.

2. Hold up the frame to the light and twist it. What do you see?

_____

3. Have your partner try to stick his or her hand through the bubble frame without breaking the bubble. What should he or she do first to make it work? (Hint: Look back at page 5.)

_____

_____

⑩ Bubble Ride (1)

1. Imagine that you are trapped inside a bubble that is floating through the air outside. Up and away you go!

2. Draw a picture that shows your imaginary adventure. On the next page, describe what's happening in the picture.

- -

⑪ Bubble Ride (2)

My Bubble Adventure

_____

_____

_____

_____

_____

_____

_____

My Five Senses

Materials

- lab book pages 82–87, reproduced and fashioned into a booklet, one per student

- page 81, reproduced as an overhead transparency

- blindfolds

- small objects (paper clips, chalk, leaves, coins, crayons, rubber bands, etc.) in pairs

- shoeboxes

- cotton balls

- extracts, assorted flavors (banana, lemon, mint, vanilla, maple)

- aluminum foil

- gumdrops, assorted flavors (lemon, lime, orange, cherry, licorice)

- liquids, assorted (sugar water, salt water, 7UP, soda water)

- trays

- cups, plastic or paper

Objectives

- identify the five senses

- use sense of sight, hearing, and smell to identify things around them

- use sense of touch to match objects blindfolded

- describe a smell that evokes a memory

- recognize the role of smell in tasting food

- conclude that senses work best when they work together

Preparation

In many of these activities, students will work with a partner. One student will be blindfolded while the other one leads him or her through an exercise. Before you begin each activity that involves the use of a blindfold, go over with students rules for safe behavior. Instruct sighted partners that they are not to put their partners in any unsafe situations, or take advantage of their condition in any way. Remind them that they will be the ones blindfolded next.

Student partners will be going to different locations around the school—the school yard, perhaps the cafeteria. Before you begin an activity that involves leaving the classroom, inform students where they are allowed to go and where they are not.

Collect an assortment of small objects in pairs. The objects should be safe to touch. No sharp tacks or sticky glue.

Soak a set of cotton balls with different extracts. Place each cotton ball on a square of aluminum foil. Label each square on the bottom with the name of the extract.

Pour a small amount of each liquid into a plastic or paper cup. Label the cups on the bottom with the names of the liquids.

Background Information

Humans employ the use of five different senses to help them gather information about their surroundings. In most cases, the senses work together to create an accurate picture of one's environment.

All animals use their senses to gather information about their environment so that they can make decisions about how to act or behave to meet their needs. For example, imagine a dog standing in a baseball field. Across the field, he sees tall objects moving and hears people laughing. Moving a bit closer, he smells the scent of grilled meat. Approaching the picnic area, he finds a piece of discarded hamburger. He pokes it with his nose, feeling its texture. He takes it in his mouth and tastes it. It is good and he eats it. The dog has used all his senses to find and ingest food. Like all animals, a dog must eat to survive. Thus, his senses help him to survive in his environment.

Assessment Ideas

Come up with a list of activities (e.g., watching a play, swimming, doing homework, baking cookies, sewing). For each activity, have students name the senses they would need to use to perform the activity.

Extension Ideas

Have students research how people with hearing or sight disabilities make up for the lack of input and are able to get around in the world. What special equipment do they use? What adjustments do they make in their daily routine?

79

Lab Book Instructions & Answers

Page 1: The five senses are sight, hearing, touch, taste, and smell. Once students have recorded their ideas, make an overhead transparency of page 81.

Page 2: Encourage students to use descriptive language.

Page 3: Show students how to properly put on a blindfold. Remind them of the safety rules associated with blindfolds. Once students have recorded their ideas and removed their blindfolds, have them check their ideas and make any corrections.

Page 4: Review procedures for using blindfolds. Once students have recorded their ideas and removed their blindfolds, have them check their ideas and make any corrections.

Page 5: Place one of each paired object in a shoebox. Leave the pairs outside the box. Each team of students will need one box and one set of matching objects. Review safety procedures for using blindfolds.

Page 6: Students will need a set of extract-soaked cotton balls on aluminum foil squares (see Preparation). Show students how to properly put on a blindfold. Remind them of the safety rules associated with blindfolds. Once students have recorded their ideas and removed their blindfolds, have them check their ideas and make any corrections.

Page 7: Student ideas will vary, but should relate a specific smell to a specific memory or place.

Page 8: Students will need a set of assorted gumdrops (see Materials). Show students how to properly put on a blindfold. Remind them of the safety rules associated with blindfolds. Once students have recorded their ideas and removed their blindfolds, have them check their ideas and make any corrections.

Page 9: Each student or group will need a set of assorted liquids in cups (see Preparation). Students should begin by looking at each liquid from a distance. They should then record their ideas about what the liquids are in the "Looking" column of the chart. They should then smell each liquid and record their ideas about what the liquids are in the "Smelling" column of the chart. They should then taste each liquid and record their ideas in the last column of the chart. Their ideas may change from one column to the next, or they may stay the same. By the time they get to the third column, their answers should be correct.

Page 10: Review procedures for using blindfolds. Show students how to hold their nostrils closed by pinching the nostrils between thumb and forefinger. Once students have recorded their ideas and removed their blindfolds, have them check their ideas and make any corrections. Students will find that, without their sense of smell to aid them, it is harder to tell one flavor from another. Tell them that the sense of smell and taste are connected.

Page 11: Students should relate examples of where they misidentified an object because one sense working alone did not gather enough information. For example, they may have misidentified some of the scents they smelled around the school because they couldn't see where they were to get visual clues about what might be producing the smells.

80

My Five Senses

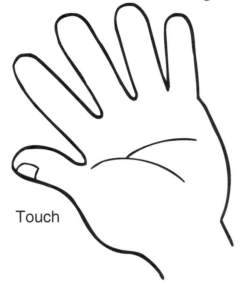

Touch

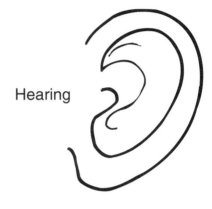

Hearing

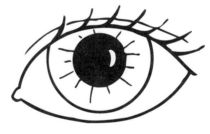

Sight

Taste

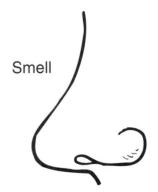

Smell

81

My Lab Book

My Five Senses

Name _____   Date _____

- -

❶
Five Senses

1. Think about how you learn about the things around you. You use your five senses to take in information.

2. Do you know what your five sense are? Sight is one of them. You learn something about objects around you by looking at them. What are your other four senses? If you don't know, take a guess.

_____

_____

_____

3. Your teacher will tell you what the other four senses are. Correct your answers above if you need to.

② What Do You See?

Use your sense of sight to describe some of the objects you can see from your seat. Describe as much about the objects as you can.

Object	Description

---

③ What Do You Hear?

1. Pick a partner. Have your partner blindfold you.

2. Go outside with your partner. What do you hear? Use your sense of hearing to find out what is going on around you.

3. Tell your partner the sounds you hear and what you think they are. Your partner will write down your ideas on the chart.

Sound	What I Think It Is

4. Switch with your partner and do the activity again.

❹
What Do You Smell?

1. Pick a partner. Have your partner blindfold you.

2. Your partner will lead you somewhere. What do you smell?
   Use your sense of smell to try to figure out where you are.

3. Tell your partner what you smell and what you think is making the
   smells. Your partner will write down your ideas on the chart.

Smell	What I Think Is Making the Smell

4. Switch with your partner and do the activity again.

- -

❺
What Do You Feel?

1. Pick a partner. Have your partner blindfold you.

2. Feel the object your partner gives you.

3. Then, using only one hand, feel the objects in the mystery box.
   Try to match the object you felt to one of the objects in the box.

4. Set each object you pick from the box next to its match.

5. When you are done matching the objects, take off your blindfold.

6. How many matches did you get right? _____

7. Switch with your partner and do the activity again.

❻ Name That Smell

1. Pick a partner. Have your partner blindfold you.

2. Your partner will have you smell five different scents. Try to name each scent. Your partner will write your ideas on the chart.

Number	Scent
1	
2	
3	
4	
5	

3. Switch with your partner and do the activity again.

- -

❼ Smell Memory

1. Many people say that smells remind them of past memories more than anything else.

2. Can you think of a smell that reminds you of a special memory or place? Maybe it's the smell of your grandma's house. Maybe it's the smell of chemicals in a pool that reminds you of summer camp.

3. Write about a smell that reminds you of a special memory.

_____

_____

_____

❽
Gumdrop Test

1. Pick a partner. Have your partner blindfold you.

2. Your partner will give you five different fruit-flavored gumdrops, one at a time. Try to name each flavor. Your partner will write your ideas on the chart.

Number	Gumdrop Flavor
1	
2	
3	
4	
5	

3. Switch with your partner and do the activity again.

- -

❾
Name That Liquid

1. Look at the tray of liquids in front of you. Record what you think they are just by looking at them.

2. Smell each liquid. Record what you think they are by looking at them and smelling them.

3. Taste each liquid. Can you tell what they are by looking at them, smelling them, and tasting them? Record your answers.

Liquid	Looking	Smelling	Tasting
1			
2			
3			
4			

⑩ Nose Plug

1. Pick a partner. Have your partner blindfold you.

2. Your partner will give you five different fruit-flavored gumdrops again. But this time, plug your nose as you eat them.

3. Try to name each flavor. Your partner will write your answers on the chart.

Number	Gumdrop Flavor
1	
2	
3	
4	
5	

4. Switch with your partner and do the activity again.

- -

⑪ Senses Work Together

1. All of your senses help you get information about the things around you. But no one sense works well all by itself.

2. Look back at the pages of your lab book. Find examples of where using more than one sense at a time would have helped you name a smell or taste or sound. Write some of your examples below.

_____

_____

_____

_____

Sink and Float

Materials

- lab book pages 91–97, reproduced and fashioned into a booklet, one per student
- assorted small objects (paper clips, buttons, corks, coins, pencils, keys, marbles, table tennis balls, small balloons)
- plastic trays
- plastic tubs
- water
- newspaper
- paper towels
- quarters
- tennis balls
- eggs, hard-boiled and shelled
- pitcher
- salt
- stirring spoon
- plastic cups
- cooking oil
- corn syrup
- plastic bottles, with caps
- sand
- funnels
- graduated cylinders
- clay
- aluminum foil

Objectives

- recall objects they have seen sink or float in water
- determine which of a set of small objects will sink or float
- recognize that objects in water push on the water, while the water pushes back on the objects
- recognize that denser liquids push harder than less dense liquids
- experiment with object shape and ability to float
- manipulate objects to make them sink or float

Preparation

Collect enough plastic tubs so that each student or group will have one to work with. Transparent tubs are better than opaque ones, but either will do.

Cover each student's or group's work area with newspapers to catch spills. This will make cleanup easier. Distribute paper towels each time the tubs of water are used.

Hard boil an egg for each student or group. Peel the eggs. Remind students that they should never eat anything in science class unless told to do so by you.

Prepare a pitcher of saltwater solution by stirring salt into the pitcher of water until the salt begins to settle at the bottom. You'll need about 3 lbs of salt per gallon of water.

Collect a graduated cylinder or other measuring container for each student or group. The container should show cc increments.

Background Information

Whether an object sinks or floats in water depends primarily on the density of the object. Simply put, if the object is more dense than water, it will sink. If the object is less dense, it will float. An object's tendency to float is called buoyancy.

An object in water exerts a downward force on the water due to its weight. The water, in turn, exerts an upward force on the object. This force is known as the buoyant force. Archimedes' principle states that the buoyant force pushing up on an object is equal to the weight of the water the object displaces, or pushes aside. Therefore, buoyancy is also influenced by the shape of the object. A ball of clay will sink because clay is denser than water. But the same ball shaped into a boat will displace more water and therefore have a greater buoyant force acting on it. This increased buoyant force allows the clay boat to float.

Whether an object sinks or floats also depends on the liquid it is placed in, as each liquid has its own density. Denser liquids may support objects that less dense liquids cannot.

89

Page 1: Students may recall seeing buoys, boats, birds, and plastic toys floating on water.

Page 2: 2) Answers will vary, but might touch on the materials each object was made of.

Page 3: Prepare a tray of small objects (see Materials List) for each student or group to make predictions about. The objects should be small enough to fit in the tubs of water you provide, and should not be damaged by water.

Page 4: 1) Answers will vary according to objects tested. 2) Answers will vary. Hold a class discussion after the experiments to compare results of groups.

Page 5: 1) Answers will vary according to objects tested. 2) Answers will vary. Hold a class discussion after the experiments to compare results of groups.

Page 6: Give each student or group a tub of water, a quarter, and a tennis ball. 1) It sinks. 2) Help students see that it pushed the water out of the way. 3) It floats. 4) The ball pushes back up on students' hands. Lead students to conclude that objects placed in water push down on the water, while the water pushes back up on the objects. They can feel this as the tennis ball resists submersion.

Page 7: Give each student or group a cup of plain water, a cup of saltwater solution, and a peeled hard-boiled egg. 2) It sinks. 3) It floats. 4) The salt water, because it pushed hard enough to support the egg and make it float. The plain water did not push hard enough, so the egg sank.

Page 8: Give each student or group a cup of plain water, a cup of cooking oil, and a cup of corn syrup. Also distribute a tray of four assorted objects to test. Answers will vary according to objects tested, but some objects may float in corn syrup while they sink in water because corn syrup is more dense than water. Cooking oil is somewhere in between. Denser liquids push up on objects harder than do less dense liquids.

Page 9: Distribute a plastic bottle with cap, a tub of water, a funnel, a graduated cylinder, and some sand to each student or group. 1) It floats. 2) air; 3) No; 5) Answers will vary. 6) All students should get approximately the same result.

Page 10: Give each student or group a piece of clay and a tub of water. 2) It sinks. 5) Students may say that flatter objects float better than balled-up objects.

Page 11: Give each student or group a piece of foil and a tub of water. 2) It sinks. 5) Students may say that, in both cases, flattening out the material and curving the ends up so water couldn't get in made it float better.

Page 12: Distribute chosen objects and a tub of water to each student or group. Encourage them to use their imagination when coming up with ideas to make their objects float. 1) I could make the object somehow push less hard on the water.

Page 13: Distribute chosen objects and a tub of water to each student or group. Encourage them to use their imaginations when coming up with ideas to make their objects sink. 1) I could make the object somehow push harder on the water.

My Lab Book
Sink and Float

Name _____ Date _____

- -

① Remember Back

1. Some objects sink in water. Others float on the water's surface.

2. Try to remember a time when you were in or near water. Maybe it was a pool, the ocean, a lake, or even a bathtub.

3. List some objects that you remember seeing sink. Then list objects you remember seeing float.

Objects That Sank	Objects That Floated

❷ Why Did They Do That?

1. Look back at the list of objects you wrote down on page 1.

2. Write down why you think each object sank or floated in the water.

Object	Why Did It Sink or Float?

- -

❸ Will They Sink or Float?

1. Look at the tray of objects in front of you. Which objects do you think will sink in water? Which do you think will float?

2. Divide the objects into two piles: a Sink pile and a Float pile. List the objects you put in each pile.

Objects I Think Will Sink	Objects I Think Will Float

❹ Does It Sink?

1. Test each of the objects in your Sink pile by putting them in a tub of water. Record what happens on the chart below.

Object	Prediction	Result

2. Which objects surprised you?

_____

_____

- -

❺ Does It Float?

1. Test each of the objects in your Float pile by putting them in a tub of water. Record what happens on the chart below.

Object	Prediction	Result

2. Which objects surprised you?

_____

❻ Pushing Match

1. Put a quarter in a tub of water. What happens to the quarter?

   _____

2. What did the quarter do to the water below it as it fell to the bottom of the tub? _____

   _____

3. Put the tennis ball in the tub. What happens to the ball?

   _____

4. Push down on the ball so that it goes under water. What do you feel?

   _____

   _____

- -

❼ Salty Water

1. On page 6, you learned that when you put an object in water, the object pushes on the water and the water pushes back on the object. Whichever object pushes harder wins. If the object pushes harder, the object sinks. If the water pushes harder, the object floats.

2. Put an egg in the cup of plain water. What happens to the egg?

   _____

3. Now put the egg in the cup of salt water. What happens to the egg? _____

4. Which pushed harder on the egg, the plain water or the salt water? How can you tell? _____

❽ Different Liquids

1. Look at the objects your teacher gives you.

2. Put each of the objects into the cup of water, one at a time. Which sank? Which floated? Record your results on the chart.

3. Repeat step 2 with the cups of cooking oil and corn syrup. Record your results.

Object	In Water	In Cooking Oil	In Corn Syrup

- -

❾ Bobbing Bottle

1. Put a capped empty bottle into a tub of water. What happens to the bottle? _____

2. What is the bottle filled with? _____

3. Use the funnel to put 10 cc of sand in the bottle. Put the cap back on. Does the bottle float now?_____

4. Keep adding sand, 10 cc at a time, until the bottle sinks.

5. How much sand did it take before the bottle sank? _____ cc

6. Compare your results with your classmates'. Did they get the same result?

_____

⑩ Clay Shapes

1. Form the clay into a ball. Put it in the tub of water.

2. What happens to the clay? _____

3. How can you make the same piece of clay float? Write your ideas below.

   _____

   _____

4. Try out your idea. Did it work? _____

5. What did you learn about what makes an object sink or float?

   _____

   _____

   _____

- -

⑪ Foil Fun

1. Crumple the sheet of foil into a ball. Put it in the tub of water.

2. What happens to the foil? _____

3. How can you make the same piece of foil float? Write your ideas below.

   _____

   _____

4. Try out your idea. Did it work? _____

5. How was this activity like the one you did with clay?

   _____

⑫ Make It Float

1. Remember that objects in water push on the water, and the water pushes back on them. Knowing this, how do you think you could make an object that sinks, float?

_____

2. Look at the objects you listed on page 4. Choose one that you would like to try to make float. What object did you choose?

_____

3. Use whatever materials you want to try to make the object float.

4. Did you get the object to float? Describe what you did.

_____

_____

_____

- -

⑬ Make It Sink

1. Remember that objects in water push on the water, and the water pushes back on them. Knowing this, how do you think you could make an object that floats, sink?

_____

2. Look at the objects you listed on page 5. Choose one that you would like to try to make sink. What object did you choose?

_____

3. Use whatever materials you want to try to make the object sink.

4. Did you get the object to sink? Describe what you did.

_____

Animal Behavior

Materials

- lab book pages 102–107, reproduced and fashioned into a booklet, one per student

- page 101, reproduced as an overhead transparency

- mealworms

- bran

- apple

- plastic containers with holes punched in lid

- snails

- lettuce leaves

- hand lenses

- shoeboxes with lids

- heating pads (or other safe heat sources)

- self-locking bags

- crushed ice

- aluminum foil

- paper towels

- water

Objectives

- draw and describe physical characteristics of mealworms and snails

- gather data on mealworm and snail preferences for warm and cool areas

- gather data on mealworm and snail preferences for light and dark areas

- gather data on mealworm and snail preferences for wet and dry areas

- observe how mealworms and snails move in search of food

- compare mealworm and snail behavior using a Venn diagram

Preparation

Purchase some mealworms from a bait shop. Store the mealworms in a plastic container with a lid. Punch holes in the lid for air. Put several cups of bran in with the mealworms. Add a small piece of apple for moisture.

Collect, or have students collect, snails from a garden. Keep the snails in a plastic container with lettuce leaves and water sprayed on the sides of the container. The environment should be moist.

Collect a number of shoeboxes with lids. Students will use the boxes and their lids in the behavior experiments.

You will need a number of heating pads or other sources of heat to place under the shoeboxes. You may choose to warm ceramic tiles in the oven and wrap them in towels. Make sure students do not touch the tiles directly. You may even be able to find a sunny spot where you can set one side of the boxes in the sun and the other out of the sun.

A day before doing the "Finding Food" activities on pages 5 and 10, remove the mealworms and snails from their food sources. This will ensure that they are hungry when they go looking for food in the experiment.

Background Information

Mealworms are not worms at all. They are the larval stage of the common darkling beetle. They are called mealworms because they resemble worms and feed on bran "meal" at this stage of life. Mealworms live in warm, dry environments. The warmth helps speed up their development process. They need a minimal amount of moisture to survive.

Snails, on the other hand, live in cool, moist conditions. You may have noticed that snails are most active during the cool night, the dewy dawn, and on rainy days. When it is dry and warm outside, snails are hiding in dark, moist places. Because their bodies (except for those parts under the shell) are vulnerable to desiccation, they can't stay in dry, warm areas for long.

Thus, mealworms and snails will act in very different ways to survive in an environment. Mealworms will seek warmth and dryness, while snails seek coolness and moisture. Both will choose darkness, the mealworm to avoid predators and the snail to avoid drying sunlight.

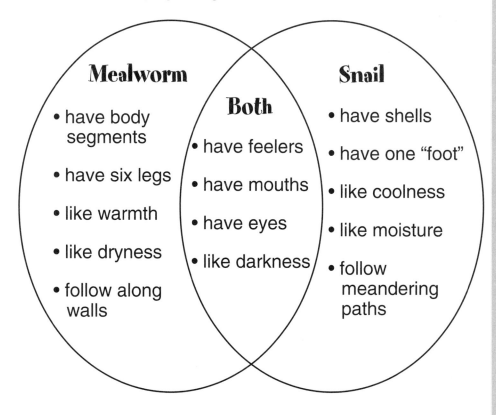

Mealworm
- have body segments
- have six legs
- like warmth
- like dryness
- follow along walls

Both
- have feelers
- have mouths
- have eyes
- like darkness

Snail
- have shells
- have one "foot"
- like coolness
- like moisture
- follow meandering paths

Lab Book Instructions & Answers

Page 1: Make an overhead transparency of the Mealworm diagram on page 101. Once students have completed their drawings, show the transparency and have students make corrections to their drawings and labels as needed. 3) six; 4) Answers will vary.

Page 2: Distribute a heating pad or other safe heat source to each student or group. Also give each group a bag of crushed ice that lies relatively flat. Have them place half of their boxes on the pad and the other half on the bag of ice so that one half of the box is warm while the other half is cool. 3) the warm side; 4) Mealworms live in warm, dry environments, so the mealworm would survive better in warm areas. The heat helps them to grow and develop into pupae.

Page 3: Distribute a sheet of foil to each student or group. The foil will go over half the shoebox. The mealworm should be placed in the center of the box, just below the edge of the foil. 3) under the foil; 4) Hiding in a dark place would keep the mealworm safe from predators. Save the foil for use again on page 8.

Page 4: Distribute a wet paper towel to each student or group. (You may want to have them place a piece of foil beneath the wet towel to keep it from damaging the cardboard box.) 3) probably to the dry side, or it may stay at the boundary; 4) Mealworms live in warm, dry environments, so they are better suited to the dry side. Their hard body coverings keep them from drying out.

Page 5: Make sure you remove the mealworms from their food source one day before you do this activity. The mealworms should eventually find the bran. They will most likely move along the walls of the box to get there.

Page 6: Make an overhead transparency of the Snail diagram on page 101. Once students have completed their drawings, show the transparency and have students make corrections to their drawings and labels as needed. 3) the shorter ones; 4) the longer ones.

Page 7: Distribute a heating pad or other safe heat source to each student or group. Also give each group a bag of ice that lies relatively flat. Have them place half of their boxes on the pad and the other half on the bag of ice so that one half of the box is warm while the other half is cool. 3) the cool side; 4) Warm environments would dry out the snail, and it would die.

Page 8: Have students use the same sheets of foil from their mealworm experiment. The snail should be placed in the center of the box, just below the edge of the foil. 3) under the foil; 4) Dark places are typically moister than areas exposed to drying sunlight.

Page 9: Distribute a wet paper towel to each student or group. (You may want to have them place a piece of foil beneath the wet towel to keep it from damaging the cardboard box.) 3) the wet side; 4) Snails need moist environments because their soft bodies are exposed and could dry out.

Page 10: Make sure you remove the snails from their food source one day before you do this activity. The snails should eventually find the lettuce. They may follow a meandering path to get there.

Page 11: Explain to students that a Venn diagram is a chart they can use to help them compare two things and see what they have in common and how they are unique. Characteristics unique to each thing are shown in the left and right ovals, while the oval intersection holds the shared characteristics. You may choose to do this exercise on the board as a class.

Mealworm

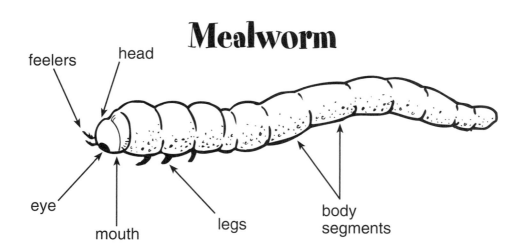

feelers   head

eye

mouth

legs

body
segments

Snail

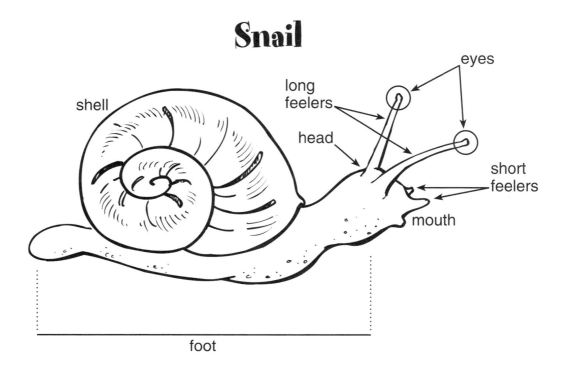

shell

eyes

long
feelers

head

short
feelers

mouth

foot

My Lab Book
Animal Behavior

Name _____ Date _____

- -

①
Observe a Mealworm

1. Use a hand lens to examine a mealworm up close. Draw and describe what you see.

2. Label its head, mouth, eyes, legs, and feelers.

3. How many legs does it have?_____

4. How many body segments does it have?_____

❷ Warm or Cold?

1. Place the mealworm in the box. Put the lid on.

2. Set half of the box on a heating pad. Set the other half on the bag of ice.

3. Which side does the mealworm go to? _____

4. How do you think the mealworm's behavior might help it to survive in its environment?

_____

_____

_____

_____

_____

- -

❸ Lightness or Darkness?

1. Cover half of the shoebox with foil.

2. Place the mealworm in the box just below the edge of the foil. Wait a few minutes.

3. Where does the mealworm go? _____

4. How do you think the mealworm's behavior might help it to survive in its environment?

_____

_____

_____

❹
Wet or Dry?

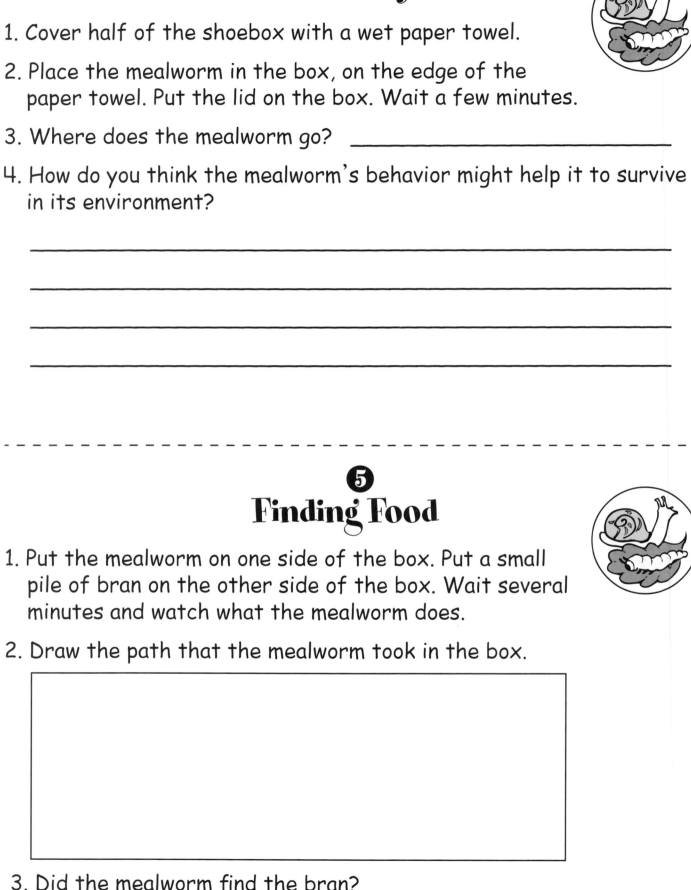

1. Cover half of the shoebox with a wet paper towel.

2. Place the mealworm in the box, on the edge of the paper towel. Put the lid on the box. Wait a few minutes.

3. Where does the mealworm go? _____

4. How do you think the mealworm's behavior might help it to survive in its environment?

_____

_____

_____

_____

- -

❺
Finding Food

1. Put the mealworm on one side of the box. Put a small pile of bran on the other side of the box. Wait several minutes and watch what the mealworm does.

2. Draw the path that the mealworm took in the box.

3. Did the mealworm find the bran? _____

❻
Observe a Snail

1. Use a hand lens to examine a snail up close. Draw and describe what you see.

2. Label its head, mouth, eyes, shell, foot, and feelers.

3. Which feelers seem to be used for feeling? _____

4. Which feelers seem to be used for seeing?_____

- -

❼
Warm or Cold?

1. Place the snail in the box. Put the lid on.

2. Set half of the box on a heating pad. Set the other half on the bag of ice.

3. Which side does the snail go to? _____

4. How do you think the snail's behavior might help it to survive in its environment?

_____

_____

_____

❽ Lightness or Darkness?

1. Cover half of the shoebox with foil.

2. Place the snail in the box just below the edge of the foil. Wait a few minutes.

3. Where does the snail go? _____

4. How do you think the snail's behavior might help it to survive in its environment?

_____

_____

_____

_____

_____

- -

❾ Wet or Dry?

1. Cover half of the shoebox with a wet paper towel.

2. Place the snail in the box, on the edge of the paper towel. Put the lid on the box. Wait a few minutes.

3. Where does the snail go? _____

4. How do you think the snail's behavior might help it to survive in its environment?

_____

_____

_____

⑩ Finding Food

1. Put the snail on one side of the box. Put a small piece of lettuce on the other side of the box. Wait several minutes and watch what the snail does.

2. Draw the path that the snail took in the box.

3. Did the snail find the lettuce? _____

- -

⑪ Compare Mealworms and Snails

1. In the left-hand oval on the Venn diagram below, list the characteristics that mealworms have but snails don't.

2. Then, in the oval on the right, list the characteristics that snails have but mealworms don't.

3. Finally, in the middle oval, list the characteristics that both mealworms and snails share.

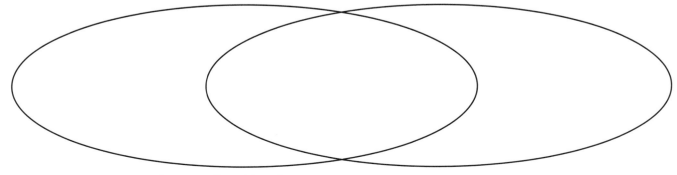

Water

Materials

- lab book pages 112–117, reproduced and fashioned into a booklet, one per student
- page 111, reproduced as an overhead transparency
- cups, plastic
- water
- waxed paper
- paper towels
- scissors
- food coloring (red, blue, or green)
- pitcher
- flour
- sugar
- sand
- talcum powder
- craft sticks
- plastic soda bottles
- aluminum foil
- graduated cylinders
- plastic wrap
- measuring tapes or yardsticks
- ice
- plastic lid
- black construction paper
- matches
- masking tape
- lamp

Objectives

- identify the ways in which they use water
- determine some of the physical properties of water
- recognize water's three physical states
- investigate the processes of evaporation and condensation
- make a model cloud
- identify components of the water cycle

Preparation

Some of the activities in this unit require wait time. Read all the pages before deciding how to best schedule the individual activities.

You will need access to a freezer for the activity on lab book page 6. Make sure there is enough room to fit each student's or group's bottle.

You will need to locate a puddle in your school yard, or create one using a garden hose. The puddle should be wide and shallow and preferably located in a sunny spot.

Background Information

Water is a polar molecule that exhibits both cohesive and adhesive properties. Cohesion is attraction between like molecules. Cohesion between water molecules allows water to stick to water. That's why water forms drops that move when pulled. Adhesion is the attraction between unlike molecules. Adhesion allows water to be pulled up the length of an absorbent paper towel.

Water moves around Earth via the water cycle. The processes of evaporation, condensation, and precipitation make up the cycle that drives water from one location to the next. Water that evaporates from lakes and oceans rises up into the atmosphere, is cooled, and condenses to form clouds. Once enough droplets have condensed, they are heavy enough to fall to Earth as precipitation. Then the cycle begins again.

Lab Book Instructions & Answers

Page 1: 1) drinking fountain, sink, bathroom, puddles, swimming pool; 2) lakes, streams, rivers, ponds, raindrops, snow, ice, puddles; 4) cooking, bathing, brushing teeth, washing dishes, washing car/pet, swimming.

Page 2: Give each student or group a cup of water and a piece of waxed paper. 2) The drop is rounded, not flat. 3) The drop moves in the direction it is pulled and stays a complete drop. 4) Water sticks to itself. When you pull some of it, the rest comes along.

Page 3: Mix up a pitcher of colored water. Cut long strips out of paper towels. Distribute a cup of colored water and a paper towel strip to each student or group. Make sure students submerge only the very edge of the strip in the water. 2) It moves up the towel. 3) Water is absorbed by some materials and can be pulled up into them.

Page 4: Put a small amount of flour, sugar, sand, and talcum powder into separate cups. Each student or group will need one set. They will also need a full cup of water and a craft stick for stirring. Distribute materials. 2) Sugar and flour will dissolve. Sand and talcum powder will not. 3) Water dissolves some materials. Tell students that water dissolves more materials than any other liquid.

Page 5: 2) water in a pond, ice in a glass of juice, steam above a pot of water on the stove; 3) water freezing in the ice cube tray, water boiling on the stove, snow melting on the lawn.

Page 6: Each student or group will need a plastic soda bottle, access to water, and a small square of foil. You will need to place all the bottles in the freezer for several hours or overnight. 4) The ice will have risen above the mouth of the bottle, poking out in a column. 5) Help students conclude that water expands (takes up more space) as it freezes.

Page 7: Distribute two plastic cups, some water, a small piece of plastic wrap, and a graduated cylinder to each student or group. Have students place their cups in a sunny location where they won't be disturbed. 3) Some of the water in the uncovered cup will have evaporated. The amount of water in the covered cup should be the same. 4) Help students to understand that the water evaporated, or became steam, and went into the air.

Page 8: Depending on the weather, students may have to observe the puddle over several days. If so, simply have them change the headings of the chart. 3) Students will witness the puddle slowly evaporating. Help them understand that as the water was heated by the sun, it evaporated into the air.

Page 9: Prepare another pitcher of colored water. Give each student or group a cup of ice and access to the pitcher. 2) Students will notice drops of water collecting on the outside of the cup. 3) No, it is clear, and the water in the cup is colored. Help students understand that the water was in the air and the coolness of the ice made it condense on the outside of the cup.

Page 10: Do this as a demonstration. Fill a plastic cup with warm water. Let it sit for a few minutes. Then pour most of the water out. Immediately place a plastic lid with ice on top over the top of the cup. Have a student hold a piece of black construction paper behind the cup so that other students can see what's happening inside the cup. Lift the lid and throw in a lit match. 2) smoke from the match, and a small cloud forming; 3) Help students identify the conditions needed to form a cloud: warm, moist air; something to cool the air; and tiny particles of dust (provided by the smoke).

Page 11: Create a water cycle model by pouring some warm water into a plastic cup, inverting another cup on top of it, taping the edges together, and then setting some ice on top of the upper cup. Place the model under a lamp to encourage evaporation of the water. Make an overhead transparency of the Water Cycle on page 111. 3) condensation occurs as droplets of water collect on the sides of the cups; precipitation occurs as the water drips off the top of the inverted cup; evaporation occurs as the water turns to steam.

Water Cycle

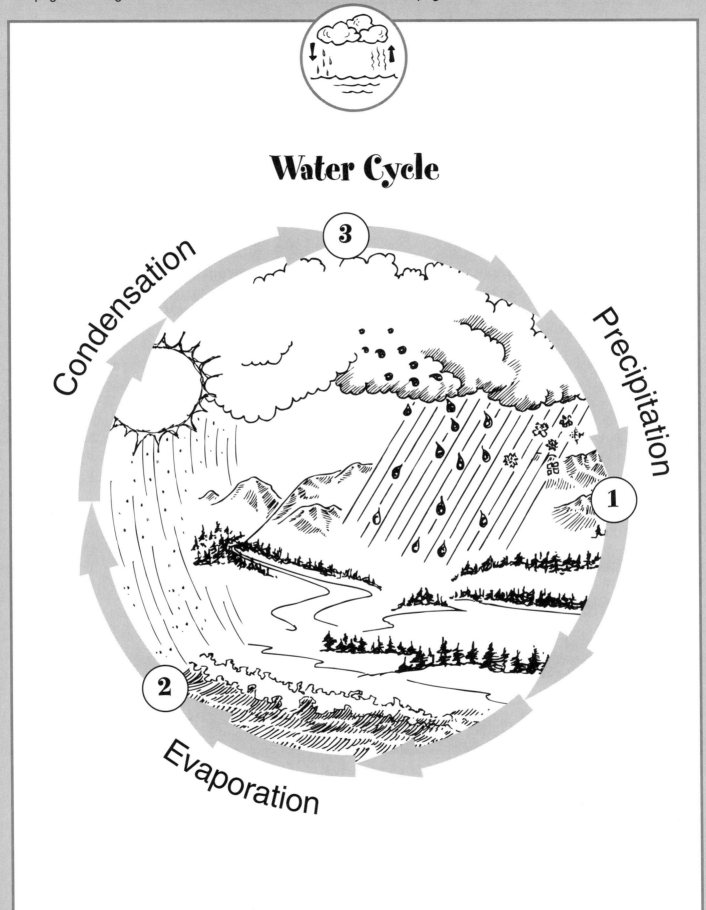

My Lab Book
Water

Name _____ Date _____

---

①
Water World

1. Water is all around you. Name some places in your school where water can be found.

   _____

   _____

2. Name some places in nature where water can be found.

   _____

   _____

3. How do you use water in your daily life? List all the ways.

   _____

   _____

❷ Waterdrops

1. Dip your finger into a cup of water. Let the drops fall onto a piece of waxed paper.

2. What do the drops look like? Draw and describe one.

_____
_____
_____

3. Stick the tip of your pencil into the drop and pull it sideways. What happens?

_____

4. Describe one property of water you observed.

_____

- -

❸ Slurp!

1. Hold a strip of paper towel just above a cup of colored water. Slowly lower the paper down so that the bottom barely touches the water. Hold it there for a minute or so.

2. Describe what the water does.

_____
_____

3. Describe one property of water you observed.

_____
_____

④ Dissolving Away

1. Look at the cups of material. What do you think will happen when you mix them with water? Write your predictions on the chart.

Material	Prediction	Result

2. Mix each cup with water. Record your results on the chart.

3. Describe one property of water you observed.

_____

- -

⑤ Three States

1. Water is a liquid. When water freezes, it becomes ice. When it boils, it becomes steam. Water, ice, and steam are the three states that water can be in.

2. Where have you seen each of these states of water? Give an example of each.

_____

_____

3. Have you ever seen water changing from one state to another? Give an example.

_____

❻
POP!-sicle

1. Fill your bottle to the top with water. Cover it with a piece of foil.

2. Draw what your bottle looks like before freezing.

Before Freezing	After Freezing

3. Put the bottle in the freezer for several hours.

4. What does your bottle look like now? Draw it above.

5. Describe one property of water you observed.

_____

- -

❼
Where Did It Go?

1. Put 30 mL of water in each cup. Cover one cup with plastic wrap. Leave the other one open.

2. Place both cups in a sunny spot. Check them the next day.

Cup	Beginning Amount (mL)	Ending Amount (mL)
With Plastic		
Without Plastic		

3. Measure the amount of water in each cup. Fill in the chart.

4. How can you explain what happened?

_____

_____

❽ Puddle Watch

1. Find a puddle in the school yard. Use a measuring tape to measure how wide it is.

2. Go back and measure it later in the day. Has the size changed? Record your results on the chart.

	Beginning	One Hour Later	Two Hours Later	Four Hours Later
Width (cm)				

3. Where did the water go?

_____

- -

❾ Water Mystery

1. Fill a cup of ice with colored water. Draw what the cup looks like.

2. Let the cup sit for several minutes. Is there anything different about the cup now? Add any changes you see.

3. Did the new water come from inside the cup? How do you know?

_____

⑩ Cloud Model

1. Watch as your teacher pours the warm water out of the cup and then puts a lid covered with ice on top of the cup. What do you see in the cup?

_____

2. Now watch as your teacher drops a match into the cup. What do you see now?

_____

3. Describe how clouds are made.

_____

_____

_____

- -

⑪ Water Cycle

1. Look at the water cycle model your teacher made.

2. Look at the overhead transparency of the Water Cycle.

3. Use the overhead to add labels that describe what is happening in the water cycle model.

Magnets

Materials

- lab book pages 121–127, reproduced and fashioned into a booklet
- small paper clips
- thread
- masking tape
- bar magnets, assorted strengths
- cloth swatches (flannel, wool)
- plastic bags
- aluminum foil
- balloons (deflated)
- buttons (metal and plastic)
- steel can lids
- pennies
- corks
- iron nails
- washers
- brass paper fasteners
- plastic spoons
- packing peanuts
- wooden blocks
- plain white paper
- iron filings
- plastic cups
- sewing needles
- plastic tubs
- water
- compasses

Objectives

- experiment to determine which objects are attracted to a magnet and which are not
- identify the poles of the magnet as the areas where magnetic force is strongest
- experiment with pole interactions
- use iron filings to show the magnetic field surrounding a magnet
- determine which objects can block the magnetic attraction between a magnet and an object
- create a temporary magnet
- construct a compass using a magnetized needle

Preparation

Prepare the floating paper clip demonstration for the class. Tie a piece of thread to a paper clip. Tape one end of the thread to a table. Wrap a magnet in paper so that students cannot see what it is.

Pour a small amount (1 to 2 Tbsp.) of iron filings into a cup for each student or group. Warn students that they should never touch the filings directly to the magnet as they are hard to remove. Once they have completed the activity, they can lift the edges of the paper and pour the filings back into their cups.

Prepare a cork for each student or group by scratching a narrow groove in the center that will accommodate the magnetized needle.

Background Information

Magnetism is created by the electrons that spin around the nuclei of atoms. This spin creates a tiny magnetic field. In most materials, the force of the atoms cancel each other out. But in magnetic objects, the atoms group together in areas called domains. Within a domain, all the atoms are aligned and so the forces work together to produce a strong magnetic field.

While the domains in objects like paper clips and iron nails are not aligned, they can become aligned in the presence of a magnet. Thus, they are attracted to magnets, and can be made into temporary magnets themselves. By stroking an iron nail with a magnet in one direction many times, you align the domains in the nail, temporarily giving it magnetic properties. When the nail is dropped, the domains lose their alignment and the nail loses its magnetic properties.

The strength of a magnet is concentrated in its poles. Magnets typically have a north pole and a south pole. The rule of magnetic attraction says that like poles of different magnets repel each other while unlike poles are attracted to one another. Iron filings sprinkled lightly over a magnet will align according to the magnet's lines of force. Thus, they can be used to show how the lines of force are arranged (more concentrated at the poles).

Because Earth itself contains large amounts of magnetic material in its core, it acts as a sort of giant magnet, with its north pole near geographic south and its south pole near geographic north. The poles of compass needles interact with the poles of Earth according to the usual rules of magnetic attraction. This interaction allows us to navigate the globe by knowing which direction is north at all times.

Page 1: Set up the demonstration. Hold the covered magnet above the clip so that the clip is suspended in the air. Make the clip move left and right. Have students try holding the magnet themselves. 3) A magnet held above the paper clip attracted the paper clip to it, making it float.

Page 2: Answers will vary, but might include refrigerator magnets; magnets on toys, electronic equipment, cabinets, and so on.

Page 3: Prepare a set of objects to test for each student or group. Include one of each of the following: cloth swatch, plastic bag, piece of aluminum foil, balloon (deflated), buttons (metal and plastic), steel can lid, penny, cork, iron nail, metal washer, brass paper fastener, plastic spoon, packing peanut, wooden block, piece of plain white paper. Each student or group will also need a magnet. 1) some metal buttons, steel can lid, iron nail, some metal washers, brass paper fasteners; 2) all others. Explain that all the objects that stick to the magnet contain iron or steel.

Page 4: Give each student or group a magnet, a small paper clip, and a tiny piece of masking tape. 4) The ends of the magnets were the strongest.

Page 5: 2) north-south and south-north stuck together; north-north and south-south pushed each other away. 3) Like poles repel. Unlike poles attract. Go over the meaning of *repel* and *attract* with students as needed.

Page 6: Distribute a magnet, a piece of white paper, a piece of tape, and a cup of iron filings to each student or group. Explain that iron filings can be used to show the force of magnetic strength around a magnet. 3) The filings are most concentrated around the poles. Explain that this is because the force is strongest here.

Page 7: Give each student or group a paper clip and two magnets of different strengths. 3) Answers will vary. 4) Answers will vary. 5) The more lines between the magnet and the clip, the greater the strength of the magnet.

Page 9: Distribute a set of the same objects used on page 3 to each student or group. They will also need a magnet. 2) Answers will vary. 3) They are either magnetic themselves, or they are thick.

Page 10: Give each student or group a nail, a magnet, and some paper clips. 2) by stroking the nail with the magnet in one direction many times; 3) No, it couldn't pick up as many paper clips.

Page 11: 3) No; 4) Yes, by dropping it.

Page 12: Give each student or group a needle, a grooved cork, a tub of water, and a compass. Explain that a compass is an instrument used to show the directions of north, south, east, and west. 3) It should line up the same way as the floating needle.

Page 13: 2) Both show which way is north.

My Lab Book
Magnets

Name _____   Date _____

- -

❶
Floating Paper Clip

1. Look at the demonstration your teacher has set up. Describe what you see.

_____

_____

2. What do you think is making the paper clip float?

_____

_____

3. What made the paper clip float?

_____

② Magnets All Around

Think about places you have seen magnets before. How were the magnets being used? List your ideas on the chart.

Where I Saw a Magnet	How It Was Being Used

③ Stick to It

1. Touch each of the objects in front of you with the magnet. Which objects stick to the magnet? Put these objects in one pile.

2. Which objects do not stick to the magnet? Put these objects in another pile. List the objects in each pile.

Stick to Magnet	Do Not Stick to Magnet

❹ North and South

1. Try to pick up the paper clip using the middle of the magnet.

2. Now try picking it up using one end of the magnet.

3. Now try using the other end of the magnet.

4. What did you find? Where is the magnet strongest?

_____

_____

5. These are the **poles** of the magnet. Use tape to label one pole "North" and the other "South."

- -

❺ Pole to Pole

1. Choose a partner to work with.

2. Bring two poles of your magnets together. Fill in the chart to show which combinations of poles produce which reactions.

Pole Combination(s)	Reaction
	Magnets stick together
	Magnets push each other away

3. Circle the correct word to show the rules of magnetic attraction.

Like poles repel/attract.   Unlike poles repel/attract.

❻ Magnetic Fields

1. Tape a magnet to your desk. Put a piece of paper over it. Sprinkle the cup of iron filings over the paper slowly.

2. Draw the pattern you see the filings make. Also draw the position of the magnet underneath. Label the poles of the magnet.

3. What connection do you see between the location of the poles and the pattern of the filings?

   _____

   _____

- -

❼ Magnet Strength (1)

1. Put a paper clip on the top line of page 8. Hold a magnet at the bottom of the page so that one of the poles faces the paper clip.

2. Slowly move the magnet up near the paper clip. Stop when the clip moves.

3. How many lines were left between the magnet and the paper clip when the clip first moved? _____

4. Repeat the experiment with the other magnet. How many lines were left with this magnet? _____

5. Which magnet is stronger? What evidence do you have?

   _____

⑧ Magnet Strength (2)

_____

_____

_____

_____

_____

_____

_____

_____

- -

⑨ What Blocks a Magnet?

1. A magnet will attract a paper clip. But what if there's something between the clip and the magnet?

2. Place each of the objects your teacher gives you between the clip and the magnet. Record your observations on the chart.

Object	Did It Block the Magnet?

3. What do all the objects that blocked the magnet have in common?

_____

Making a Magnet (1)

1. Can you make a nail into a magnet? Experiment with a magnet and a nail to see if you can get the nail to pick up a paper clip.

2. How did you make the nail into a magnet?

_____

_____

_____

3. Is your nail-magnet as strong as your other magnet? How can you tell?

_____

_____

_____

- -

Making a Magnet (2)

1. Do you think you can "demagnetize" your magnet? Your nail?

2. Try some ideas.

3. Were you able to demagnetize the magnet? How?

_____

_____

4. Were you able to demagnetize the nail? How?

_____

_____

Making a Compass (1)

1. Magnetize a needle by stroking it with a magnet in one direction many times.

2. Set the needle into the groove in the cork.

3. Float the cork in a tub of water. Which direction does the needle point? Draw a picture on page 13 that shows your experiment.

4. Now set a real compass down next to your tub of water. What do you notice about the compass needle?

   _____

5. Add the compass to your drawing. Show which way the compass needle is pointing.

- -

Making a Compass (2)

1. Draw your compass experiment.

2. How is your compass like a real compass?

   _____

   _____

Plants

Materials

- lab book pages 131–137, reproduced and fashioned into a booklet

- diagram on page 129, reproduced as an overhead transparency

- lima beans

- corn kernels

- newspaper

- cups, paper or foam

- potting soil

- water

- cups, plastic

- paper towels

Objectives

- dissect and label the parts of a seed

- experiment to determine the effect of light on plant health

- experiment to determine the effect of water on plant health

- recognize that plant roots grow down and stems grow up regardless of plant orientation

- identify some of the needs of plants

Preparation

Soak a number of lima beans and corn kernels in water overnight before starting the first activity. If you are using fresh corn, do not soak the kernels. Each student will need one of each seed.

Set aside an area of the classroom where students can work with soil and water. You might want to cover the area with newspaper, set out a few bags of potting soil and a few pitchers of water, and let students come to prepare their planter cups a few at a time.

Locate a sunny spot where students can set their cups with seeds for 15 days. Also locate a dark closet where students can set their cups for 15 days.

Soak a number of lima beans before the activity on page 10.

Background Information

The seeds used in this unit are from flowering plants. Flowering plants produce seeds. Each seed is a tiny plant that can germinate to become a new plant under the right conditions.

A seed consists of a seed coat, a food supply, and an embryo plant. The seed coat's job is to keep the embryo and its food safe from the outside world. Its tough, waxy construction allows it to act as a barrier to the elements. Many seeds must be soaked in water before their seed coat will soften and split, allowing the seedling to emerge.

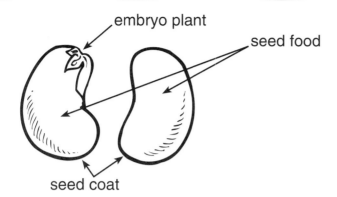

Most seeds do not need sunlight to germinate. Almost all, however, need water. Some seeds require special circumstances to begin the germination process, including heating by fire and passing through the intestinal tract of an animal.

Plants do need sunlight to grow, however. They use the energy in sunlight to produce their own food. Without sunlight, plants are unable to make their own food and soon die. Plants deprived of sunlight will become "leggy" as they put all their energy into growing tall in the hopes of finding sunlight.

Plants also need water to grow. Water is one of the components of photosynthesis. In photosynthesis, water (H_2O) and carbon dioxide (CO_2) are combined in the presence of light energy to form glucose ($C_6H_{12}O_6$) and oxygen (O_2).

$$6CO_2 + 6H_2O \longrightarrow C_6H_{12}O_6 + 6O_2$$

Water also acts as a solvent, allowing the transportation of nutrients from the soil in through the plant's roots, and all around the plant.

Gravitropism is the growth of plants in response to gravity. A plant lying on its side will soon redirect its roots to grow downward, toward the center of Earth. It does this in response to the pull of gravity, which it senses. This behavior helps a plant to survive as the best bet for a water source is toward Earth's center (underground). Conversely, plant stems will use gravity to determine which direction is up. The best bet for sunlight is "up."

129

Lab Book Instructions & Answers

Page 1: Give each student a soaked lima bean and a soaked corn kernel. 1) seeds; 3) The coat is waxy and tough. Discuss with students the role of the seed coat and how its texture helps it do its job. 4) Help students, as needed, to locate the embryo. Show and discuss the overhead transparency of page 129 to confirm that students have correctly located and labeled the parts of the seed.

Page 2: Give each student or group two paper or foam cups. Show them how to use their pencils to poke drainage holes in the bottom of the cups, or do this step yourself before distributing the cups. They will also need two lima beans and access to the soil and water. Remind students to label their cups as directed.

Page 3: The seedlings should just be emerging from the soil in both cups. Seeds do not need sunlight to germinate.

Page 4: The seedling in the sun should be doing well. The one in the dark may not be as tall or as green as the other one.

Page 5: The seedling in the sun should be healthy. The other seedling may be leggy (tall and spindly) and pale. It may even have died.

Page 6: Give each student or group two paper or foam cups. Show them how to use their pencils to poke drainage holes in the bottom of the cups, or do this step yourself before distributing the cups. They will also need two lima beans and access to the soil and water. Remind students to label their cups as directed.

Page 7: Both seedlings should be emerging from the soil surface. One initial watering should be enough to germinate the seed.

Page 8: The watered seedling should be growing strong. The unwatered seedling should be showing signs of stress.

Page 9: The watered seedling should still be growing strong. The unwatered seedling is probably dead.

Page 10: Give each student or group three soaked lima beans, a plastic cup, and two wet paper towels. Make sure that students place the seeds in different positions—some with the pinched side up, some with the pinched side down, and some with the pinched side facing sideways.

Page 11: All the seeds should have roots growing down and stems growing up, regardless of the seed orientation.

Page 12: 1) No; 2) Answers will vary. 3) All roots are growing down; all stems are growing up. 4) Plant roots find "down" no matter how they are planted. Plant stems find "up" no matter how they are planted.

Page 13: 1) Plants need sunlight and water to be healthy. 2) Plants grown in darkness died. Plants grown without water died. 3) Answers will vary, but might include air, wind, food, noise, etc.

My Lab Book
Plants

Name _____   Date _____

- -

❶
What's in a Seed?

1. Look at the two seeds in front of you. Use your fingernail to take off the seed coats.

2. How is the seed coat different from the material inside the coat?

   _____

3. Can you find the embryo plant (sprout) inside the lima bean seed?

4. Draw a picture of your lima bean seed. Label the seed coat and the embryo plant.

❷ Light and Dark (1)

1. Write your name on each of your two cups. Then label one "Light" and the other "Dark."

2. Fill the two cups with soil. The cups should be about ²/₃ full.

3. Put a seed about ¹/₃ inch below the soil surface in each cup. Pat the soil surface down gently. Pour water gently over the soil until it runs out the bottom of the cups.

4. Place one cup in a sunny spot. Place the other one in a dark closet. Water both cups every few days as needed.

5. Observe the cups over the next 15 days. Record your observations on pages 3 through 5.

- -

❸ Light and Dark (2)

Draw what you see in each of the cups after 5 days.

In the Light	In the Dark

④

Light and Dark (3)

Draw what you see in each of the cups after 10 days.

| In the Light | In the Dark |

- -

⑤

Light and Dark (4)

Draw what you see in each of the cups after 15 days.

| In the Light | In the Dark |

❻ Water and No Water (1)

1. Write your name on each of your two cups. Then label one "Water" and the other "No Water."

2. Fill the two cups with soil. The cups should be about ²⁄₃ full.

3. Put a seed about ¹⁄₃ inch below the soil surface in each cup. Pat the soil surface down gently. Pour water gently over the soil until it runs out the bottom of the cups.

4. Place both cups in a sunny spot. Water the "Water" cup every few days as needed. Do **not** water the "No Water" cup.

5. Observe the cups over the next 15 days. Record your observations on pages 7 through 9.

- -

❼ Water and No Water (2)

Draw what you see in each of the cups after 5 days.

Water	No Water

⑧
Water and No Water (3)

Draw what you see in each of the cups after 10 days.

Water	No Water

- -

⑨
Water and No Water (4)

Draw what you see in each of the cups after 15 days.

Water	No Water

⑩ Upside Down (1)

1. Line a plastic cup with a wet paper towel.

2. Place a few seeds between the towel and the cup. Spread them out and turn them in all different directions.

3. Crumple up another wet paper towel. Stick it in the middle of the cup to hold the seeds in place.

4. Place the cup in a sunny spot.

5. Every few days, look at the stems and roots that are growing from the seeds. On page 11, draw pictures of what you see.

- -

⑪ Upside Down (2)

Draw what you see in the cup after 5, 10, and 15 days.

After 5 Days	After 10 Days	After 15 Days

⑫ Upside Down (3)

1. Did the position of the seeds in the cup make a difference in the way that the stems and roots grew?

   _____

2. Turn the cup on its side. In what position do you think the stems and roots will be a few days from now?

   _____

3. Observe the cup a few days later. In which direction are the stems and roots growing? _____

4. What can you conclude about how plant stems and roots grow?

   _____

   _____

- -

⑬ Plant Needs

1. What can you conclude about the needs of plants? What two things do plants need to survive?

   _____

2. What evidence do you have for your answer?

   _____

   _____

   _____

3. If you could do another experiment to determine the needs of plants, what would you look at?

   _____

Color

Materials

- lab book pages 142–147, reproduced and fashioned into a booklet, one per student
- page 141, reproduced as an overhead transparency
- crayons, assorted colors
- plastic cups
- food coloring (red, yellow, blue)
- droppers
- waxed paper
- toothpicks
- paper towels
- white paper
- colored cellophane filters (red, yellow, blue)
- colored paper (red, yellow, blue)

Objectives

- experiment with mixing color pigments
- use paper chromatography to separate color pigments
- experiment with mixing colored filters
- investigate the interaction between colored filters and colored paper
- apply their knowledge of color mixing to solve a puzzle
- experiment with "after images"

Preparation

Each student will need one box of crayons. The box must include red, yellow, blue, green, orange, and purple crayons.

Cut several long strips of paper toweling, one strip per student.

Collect red, yellow, and blue cellophane filters. Your school's drama department is a good place to look as these filters are used for dramatic lighting.

Background Information

White light from the sun contains all the colors of the rainbow. When white light strikes an object, the object absorbs some of those colors and reflects others. (Which colors it reflects or absorbs depends on the pigments that the object contains.) The colors of light reflected by the object are the colors we see. Thus, a red apple reflects only red light. It absorbs all other colors.

Red, yellow, and blue are the primary colors of pigment. (More technically, they are magenta, yellow, and cyan, but for our purposes we will use red, yellow, and blue.) When two primary colors of pigment are mixed, they produce a new color. The color wheel describes the secondary colors created when primary colors of pigment are combined (see page 141). The mixing of pigments is known as subtractive color mixing. That's because each additional pigment absorbs new colors of light and prevents them from being reflected and therefore seen. Each new pigment subtracts from the colors we see. Overlapping colored filters is another example of subtractive color mixing, as each filter subtracts more colors of light.

Mixed color pigments can be separated using a process called paper chromatography. This technique takes advantage of the fact that different pigments have different weights. As water moves through a mixture of pigments painted onto an absorbent material, the water carries the pigments different distances according to their weights. Thus, lighter pigments are carried farther than heavier pigments.

The primary colors of light are red, blue, and green. Our eyes contain receptor cells for each of these colors. The receptors send color information to the brain, and the brain combines the information to see the color of an object. When our eyes stare at one color for a long period of time, the receptor cells in charge of reporting that color to the brain get tired. When we look away, we often see a combination of the other two colors of light. For example, when we stare at a red object for a long time, we see blue-green when we turn our eyes to a white surface. Once the red receptor cells have rested, they continue sending "red" messages to the brain, and the brain sees true color (or lack of color in the case of a white surface) again.

Extension Ideas

Have students experiment with mixing primary colors of light. Do this by covering flashlights with cellophane filters and shining the primary colors onto a blank, light-colored wall. They will notice that red, blue, and green light together appear white. That's because they are the three primary colors that make up white light.

Page 1: Give each student a box of crayons. 2) Answers will vary.

Page 2: Make sure students color each section correctly. Coloring with a light touch is necessary.

Page 3: 1) purple; 2) green; 3) orange.

Page 4: Give each student or group three plastic cups; red, blue, and yellow food coloring bottles; three toothpicks; a piece of waxed paper; and access to water.

Page 5: Red and yellow make orange. Red and blue make purple. Blue and yellow make green. 2) six. Make an overhead transparency of the art on page 141. Show students how the wheel can be used to show which color will result when any two primary colors of pigment are combined.

Page 6: Distribute a cup of water and a strip of paper toweling to each student or group. If they do not still have their materials from page 5, redistribute food coloring, toothpicks, and waxed paper. Instruct students to hold the paper towel so that the purple dot is above the water.

Page 7: 1) The water moves through the dot, carrying the blue higher up on the toweling than the red. 2) blue and red; 3) Students should be able to separate all three colors again using paper chromatography.

Page 8: Give each student or group a sheet of white paper and three colored filters—red, yellow, blue. The paper will look red through the red filter, yellow through the yellow filter, and blue through the blue filter. 2) red light; the paper looked red through the filter.

Page 9: Distribute a sheet of red, a sheet of yellow, and a sheet of blue paper to each student or group. If they do not still have their materials from page 8, redistribute the colored filters.

	Red Paper	Yellow Paper	Blue Paper
Red Filter	red	orange	purple
Yellow Filter	orange	yellow	green
Blue Filter	purple	green	blue

3) Red and yellow made orange in both cases. Red and blue made purple in both cases. Blue and yellow made green in both cases.

Page 10: Give each student a red, yellow, and blue crayon. They will also need a red, blue, and yellow filter. Heart: blue; Bunny: yellow; Mouse: red.

Page 11: Give each student a red crayon. 2) Answers will vary. Some students may say they will see it as red. 3) The sign looks blue-green. Explain how the red receptor cells in their eyes are tired by staring at red, and how the other two primary colors of light take over.

Color Wheel

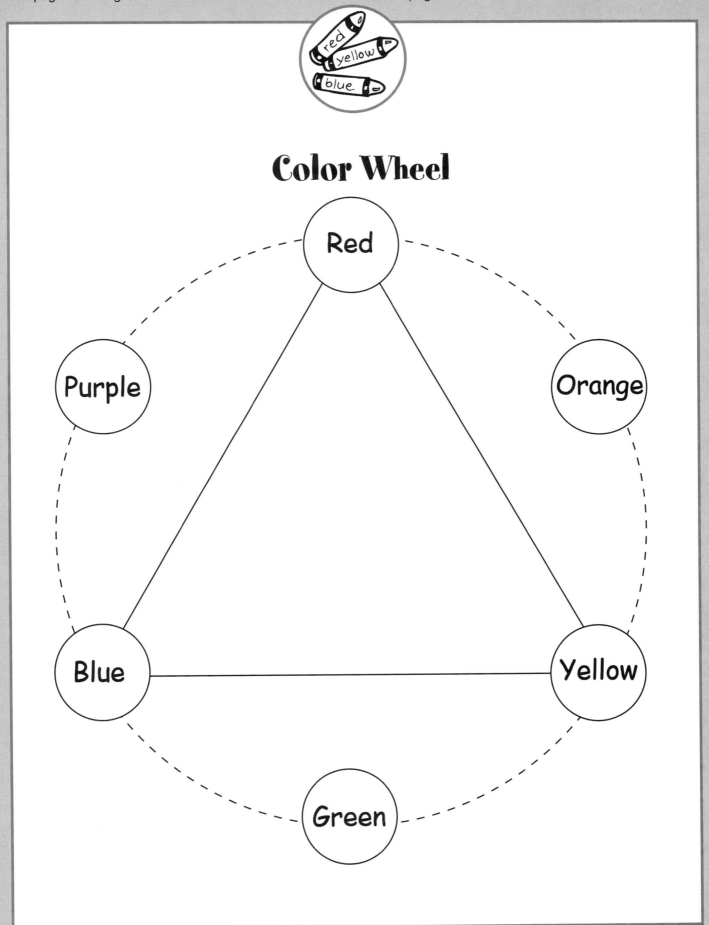

141

My Lab Book
Color

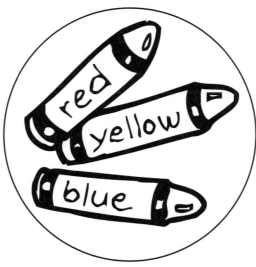

Name _____ Date _____

- -

❶
Paint a Picture

1. Color in the scene below.

2. What colors did you use in your picture?

_____

_____

_____

_____

_____

_____

_____

② Color Cross (1)

Lightly color the labeled rectangles across and down.

	red ↓	blue ↓	yellow ↓
red →			
blue →			
yellow →			

---

③ Color Cross (2)

1. Now connect the x's on page 2 using the red, blue, and yellow crayons. Use the sides of the crayons and rub lightly.

2. What color do you see where the blue and red lines cross?

_____

3. What color do you see where the blue and yellow lines cross?

_____

4. What color do you see where the yellow and red lines cross?

_____

④
Mixing Colors (1)

1. Fill three plastic cups half full with water.

2. Add two drops of red food coloring to one cup of water. Stir.

3. Do the same with two other cups of water and the yellow and blue food coloring. You should now have one cup of red water, one cup of blue water, and one cup of yellow water.

4. Mix together two drops of each water color on a piece of waxed paper.

5. What new colors did you make? Record your results on the chart on page 5.

- -

⑤
Mixing Colors (2)

1. Record the result of your color mixing experiments on the chart.

Color Combination	Result
Red and Yellow	
Red and Blue	
Blue and Yellow	

2. How many different colors of water do you have now? _____

⑥ Separating Colors (1)

1. Do you think you could separate the red and blue colors back out from the purple color you created? How? Write your ideas below.

_____

_____

2. Put one drop of red food coloring and one drop of blue food coloring on a piece of waxed paper. Mix with a toothpick.

3. Use the toothpick to paint a purple dot near the middle of a paper towel strip. Hold the bottom of the strip in a cup of water.

- -

⑦ Separating Colors (2)

1. What happens as water is soaked up into the paper towel?

_____

_____

2. What colors do you see on the paper towel? _____

3. Try the experiment again using three colors. Record what happened below.

_____

_____

❽ Color Filters (1)

1. Look at a sheet of white paper through each colored filter. What color does the paper appear to be? Record your results on the chart.

	Through Red Filter	Through Yellow Filter	Through Blue Filter
Appearance of White Paper			

2. The red filter lets only one color of light pass through it. What color do you think that is? Explain your reasoning.

_____

_____

- -

❾ Color Filters (2)

1. Try looking through the colored filters again, but this time look at colored paper.

2. What colors do the sheets of paper appear to be? Record your results on the chart.

	Red Paper	Yellow Paper	Blue Paper
Red Filter			
Yellow Filter			
Blue Filter			

3. Look back at page 5. What connection do you see between the information on that chart and the information on this chart?

_____

⑩ Colored Images

Use what you learned about color filters to decide what color crayon to use for each picture. Then try your idea to see if it is correct.

	Filter Color	Crayon Color	Color That Picture Should Appear Through Filter
Heart	Red		Purple
Bunny	Blue		Green
Mouse	Yellow		Orange

- -

⑪ After Images

1. Use a red crayon to color in the first STOP sign.

2. What do you think will happen if you stare at the red STOP sign for a long time, then look at the blank STOP sign?

_____

3. Stare at the red STOP sign for a minute. Then look at the blank STOP sign. What do you see?

_____

Life Cycles

Materials

- lab book pages 153–157, reproduced and fashioned into a booklet, one per student

- pages 151 and 152, reproduced as overhead transparencies

- pea plant seeds, several packages

- plastic planting cups with drainage holes

- newspaper

- gravel

- potting soil

- trowels

- water

- masking tape

- permanent ink marker

- rulers

- mealworms

- bran

- apple

- plastic containers with holes punched in lid

- shoebox lids

- hand lenses

Objectives

- recognize that only living things have life cycles

- grow pea plants and observe each stage of their life cycle

- raise darkling beetles (mealworms) and observe each stage of their life cycle

- recognize that, in each case, the stages form a continuous cycle

Preparation

Due to the natural development schedules of the pea plants and mealworms, you will need to conduct this unit over the course of six weeks or so. Just store the lab books in a safe place and have students pull out the books as needed.

Buy several packages of garden peas from a nursery. The fastest growing varieties are the best choice. Soak the seeds in water overnight before students plant them. This will help speed up the germination process.

Also collect a number of plastic planting containers with drainage holes. (Because the plants will be growing for several weeks, small paper cups will not be adequate.) You may be able to get your local nursery to donate these to your class as they are relatively inexpensive and nurseries use a lot of them.

Set up a distribution station with a bag of gravel, a bag of potting soil, several trowels, and a pitcher of water. Cover the station area with newspaper for easy cleanup.

Locate an area (inside is OK, but outdoors is preferred) that receives good sunlight. Students will leave their pea plants here to grow. Make sure the area is secure.

Purchase some mealworms from a bait shop. Store them in a plastic container with a lid. Punch holes in the lid for air. Put several cups of bran in with the mealworms. Add a small piece of apple for moisture.

Background Information

All living things go through a cycle of growth, reproduction, and death. In this unit, students examine the life cycle stages of a flowering plant (garden pea plant) and an insect (darkling beetle). The life cycle of the insect is somewhat unique in that it involves the process of metamorphosis. In complete metamorphosis, the organism moves through several distinct stages, where one stage looks and acts completely different from the others.

The pea plant starts out as a pea seed. When planted, the seed will germinate, grow, and develop into an adult plant. This plant will self- or cross-pollinate and form seed pods. Once dry, these seeds can be used to produce new pea plants.

The darkling beetle is an insect that undergoes complete metamorphosis. It begins as a tiny egg and hatches into a mealworm (larva) that eats and grows rapidly. The well-nourished mealworm then enters its so-called "dormant stage" and becomes a pupa. Although the pupa appears inactive, many changes are occurring inside its body. It is changing its form entirely to become an adult beetle. A few weeks later, the beetle will emerge. When adult beetles mate, they produce eggs that continue the cycle.

Assessment Ideas

Have students fill in a Venn diagram to show how each life cycle studied is unique and what both have in common.

Page 1: 2) butterflies, worms, monkeys, trees, mushrooms, bacteria; 3) They are all alive, living things.

Page 2: Invite students to come to the distribution center and prepare their planters. Then lead them to the place where they will leave their planters.

Page 3: Have students draw their plants. 1) when the seedlings are about 1 week old; 2) when flowers appear on the plants; and 3) when seed pods form on the plants. These should occur roughly 10 days, 25 days, and 42 days after planting.

Page 4: Have students complete this page once flowers have appeared on their plants. Wait until the flowers are mature and some have even lost their petals. Distribute hand lenses. 1) Answers will vary. 2) Answers will vary, but about 25 days. 3) Help students identify the pistil, stamen, and ovary if desired. 4) Students may know that flowers produce seeds. They may even be able to observe some tiny pods forming at the base of mature flowers.

Page 5: Have students complete this page once seed pods have appeared on their plants. Make an overhead transparency of the Pea Plant Life Cycle on page 151. 1) peas (seeds); 2) Students may know that they will grow into new plants. 3) The baby plant grows into an adult plant that makes flowers, that produce seeds, that grow into new plants.

Page 6: Place a mealworm and a pile of bran on an inverted shoebox lid, one for each student or group. Distribute hand lenses. 2) The mealworm is fairly active, eating bran and moving around. It moves using the six little legs near its head. Explain that the mealworm is the larval stage of the life cycle.

Page 7: Have students complete this page once the mealworms have entered their pupa stage. (They will be pale yellow, short and thick, and not moving. See picture on page 152.) Distribute hand lenses. 1) It looks different. It is shorter and thicker and paler. 3) It doesn't move at all.

Page 8: Have students complete this page once the mealworms have entered their adult stage (beetles). Distribute hand lenses. 1) It now looks like a beetle. 3) It moves around a lot and really fast. It has six big legs.

Page 9: You may choose to have students try to look for eggs. Explain what *mating* is. Make an overhead transparency of the Mealworm Life Cycle on page 152. 2) Students may know that they will hatch into tiny mealworms. 3) The mealworm turns into a pupa, which turns into an adult beetle, which lays eggs that hatch and make more mealworms. Introduce the term *metamorphosis*.

Pea Plant Life Cycle

seed

sprouting seed

seed pods

seedling

mature plant with seed pods

mature plant

mature plant with flowers

151

Mealworm Life Cycle

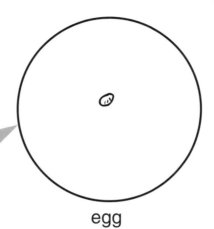

egg

adult (beetle)

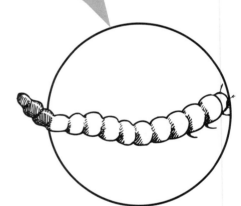

larva
(mealworm)

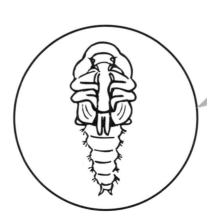

pupa

152

My Lab Book

Life Cycles

Name _____ Date _____

- -

①
Things with Life Cycles

1. A life cycle is all the different stages something goes through as it is born, grows, reproduces, and dies.

2. What sorts of things have life cycles? Circle the things below that you think have life cycles.

butterflies	cars	worms
bricks	clouds	monkeys
trees	mushrooms	bacteria

3. What do all the things you circled have in common?

_____

② Planting Pea Seeds

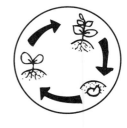

1. One group of things that have life cycles is plants. You will grow a plant and see all the different stages of its life cycle.

2. Put some gravel in the bottom of your planter. Then fill the planter about 2/3 full with soil. Use masking tape to label your container with your name.

3. Place three pea seeds on the soil. Sprinkle more soil on top and pat down. Gently pour water on the soil until it runs out the bottom of the planter.

4. Put your planter in a spot that gets sunlight every day.

- -

③ Plant Growth

Observe your planter every few days for several weeks. Draw what your pea plant looks like each time your teacher tells you to. Measure your plant and tell how tall the plant is at each stage.

Days Since Planting: ___	Days Since Planting: ___	Days Since Planting: ___

❹ Looking at Flowers

1. How many flowers are on your pea plant?_____

2. How many days did it take for the flowers to appear? _____

3. Pick off one flower from your plant. Gently pull it apart and use a hand lens to look inside. Draw what you see.

4. Why do you think plants make flowers? _____

_____

- -

❺ Pea Plant Life Cycle

1. Pull off one of the pods from your pea plant. Open it up. What do you see? _____

2. What do you think would happen if you planted one of these?

_____

3. Look at the diagram your teacher shows you. A cycle is something that repeats itself over and over. How do the stages of the pea plant make a cycle?

_____

_____

_____

❻ Meet the Mealworm

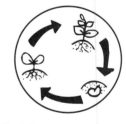

1. Look at the mealworm your teacher gives you.

2. The mealworm is in the larva stage of its life cycle. Use your hand lens to get a closer look. Draw what it looks like.

3. Describe your mealworm's activity. How does it move around?

_____

_____

_____

- -

❼ It's a Pupa

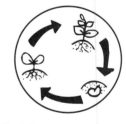

1. Look at your mealworm. How has it changed?

_____

2. Your mealworm has entered the next stage of its life cycle—the pupa stage. Use your hand lens to get a closer look. Draw your mealworm in its pupa stage.

3. Describe the pupa's activity.

_____

_____

❽ Beetle Bug

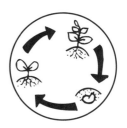

1. What does your mealworm look like now? How has it changed?

   _____

2. Your mealworm has entered the last stage of its life cycle—the adult stage. Use your hand lens to get a closer look. Draw your mealworm in its adult stage.

3. Describe the adult's activity. How does it move around?

   _____

   _____

   _____

- -

❾ Mealworm Life Cycle

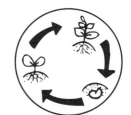

1. Adult beetles mate with each other and then lay tiny white eggs too small for you to see.

2. What do you think will happen to these eggs?

   _____

3. Look at the diagram your teacher shows you. A cycle is something that repeats itself over and over. How do the stages of the mealworm make a cycle?

   _____

   _____

   _____

Rocks and Soil

Materials

- lab book pages 162–167, reproduced and fashioned into a booklet, one per student
- pages 161 and 166 (activity 8, soil layers), reproduced as overhead transparencies
- rocks, assorted
- igneous rock (obsidian or pumice)
- sedimentary rock (sandstone)
- metamorphic rock (marble or quartzite)
- potting soil
- local soil
- plastic cups
- newspaper
- hand lenses
- tablespoons
- plastic tubes with caps
- water
- black construction paper
- dead leaves
- fresh leaves
- grass clippings
- plastic spoons
- glass jars
- tape
- plastic wrap
- earthworms

Objectives

- observe and describe characteristics of different rocks
- identify samples of the three basic types of rock
- use layering tubes to compare two soil samples
- experiment to determine where the rock pieces in soil come from
- experiment to determine where the organic matter in soil comes from
- observe the action of earthworms in soil

Preparation

Collect a wide variety of rock samples, including obsidian or pumice, sandstone, and marble or quartzite. You can collect these outside with students, or borrow some from a high school geology teacher. Each student or group will need five samples.

Buy a bag of potting soil that is rich in organic nutrients. It should not be sterile. Collect soil from somewhere around your school. Try to find soil that is noticeably different in texture and color from the potting soil.

You will need to purchase or borrow plastic layering tubes. These are tall, narrow tubes with caps (see page 166, activity 8). Wider tubes will not show the different layers of soil as clearly. Set up a distribution center where students can fill their tubes with soil and water. Cover the area with newspaper for easy cleanup.

Collect piles of fresh leaves, dried leaves, grass clippings, and any other plant matter you'd like. Make sure it's thin enough to start decomposing in a few weeks.

Purchase several dozen earthworms from a bait shop. Set up a distribution center with glass jars, soil, earthworms, black construction paper, plastic wrap, and tape.

Background Information

Rocks are made up of combinations of different minerals. There are three basic types of rock—sedimentary, igneous, and metamorphic—defined according to how they were formed. (See diagram on page 161.)

Soil is made up of rock pieces (the smallest of which is clay, the largest of which is sand or gravel), air, water, and organic matter (decaying plant and animal matter). The best soils have a high organic-matter content. These materials bring nutrients to the soil. The large pieces also promote the circulation of air and water in the soil. Earthworms also promote the circulation of water and air by burrowing tunnels. The rocky material found in soil is produced by weathering, or the breakdown of larger rocks into smaller ones by physical or chemical means.

Page 1: 1) around school or home, in a quarry, at the beach, at a lake; 2) Make sure students understand that sand is a type of rock. 3) build houses or roofs, decorate landscape, make glass (sand).

Page 2: Distribute a set of rocks to each student or group. Encourage them to be as specific as possible in their descriptions.

Page 3: Make an overhead transparency of Rock Types on page 161. Give each student or group one piece of obsidian or pumice, one piece of sandstone, and one piece of marble or quartzite. 2) obsidian or pumice; Lead students to see that obsidian is sleek and black and looks like it was once liquidy, and pumice is full of holes that might have formed as gases in the molten lava expanded during eruption.

Page 4: Give each student or group one piece of obsidian or pumice, one piece of sandstone, and one piece of marble or quartzite. 1) the sandstone, because it is made up of tiny particles cemented together; 3) marble or quartzite, because it is glassy and hard and may show crystals.

Page 5: 1) park, forest, field, yard; 2) plants and animals, dead leaves and rocks; 3) Answers will vary. Accept all answers for now.

Page 6: Give each student or group a cup of potting soil, a cup of local soil, a sheet of newspaper, and a hand lens. 2) The potting soil is a dark, rich color. It is light and moist and has little bits of plant material in it. The local soil will probably be denser and drier and have less organic matter.

Page 7: Have students come up to the distribution station a few at a time. Have them place their tubes in an undisturbed area overnight. 4) The soil in each tube has settled into different layers.

Page 8: The potting soil should show a layer of sandy material, a layer of silt, a layer of clay, and a thick layer of organic material on top. It will also have many air bubbles. (Air is one component of soil.) The local soil will probably show the same layers, but with less organic material and fewer bubbles.

Page 9: 1) sand, silt, clay, plant material, air, and water. Distribute two pieces of sandstone and a sheet of black construction paper to each student or group. 3) bits of sand; 4) Rocks rub together and small pieces of them break off.

Page 10: 1) Answers will vary, but most students know that most plants and animals live and die near and in soil. Distribute cups of soil, plastic spoons, and bits of plant material to each student or group. 4) The plant material has started to break down into smaller bits and work itself into the soil. Explain to students that this plant material is rich in nutrients and makes the soil richer and better for growing plants.

Page 11: Send students to the distribution station in small groups to assemble their jars. 4) The earthworms have burrowed through the soil, leaving tunnels. Remind students that air is an important part of soil, and tunneling helps work air into the soil. It also allows water to move around.

See page 160 "Page 3" for instructions on how to use the art on this page.

Rock Types

Sedimentary rock

forms when small bits of rock fall to the bottom of lakes or oceans. Over time, they are pressed and cemented together under their own weight.

Igneous rock

forms when molten magma from deep inside Earth comes near the surface and cools to form rock. Sometimes, the magma shoots out of a volcano in an eruption.

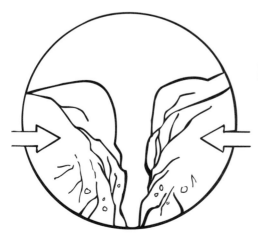

Metamorphic rock

forms when existing rocks are heated and pressed deep inside Earth. This heat and pressure changes their texture and structure.

My Lab Book
Rocks and Soil

Name _____ Date _____

---

❶
Rocks All Around

1. Describe some of the different places you have seen rocks and what the rocks looked like.

_____

_____

2. What was the biggest rock you ever saw? What was the smallest?

_____

3. How do people use rocks? Name some different ways.

_____

_____

➋ Describe Rocks

Look at the collection of rocks your teacher gives you. Describe each one. Some properties you might consider include weight, color, texture make-up, and hardness.

Rock	Properties
1	
2	
3	
4	
5	

➌ Rock Types (1)

1. Look at the overhead transparency. It shows the three basic rock types and how each one is formed.

2. Look at the three rocks in front of you. Which one do you think is igneous? Why do you think so?

_____

_____

_____

3. Were you right? _____

❹ Rock Types (2)

1. Look at the three rocks in front of you. Which one do you think is sedimentary? Why do you think so?

_____

_____

_____

2. Were you right? _____

3. Which one do you think is metamorphic? Why do you think so?

_____

_____

4. Were you right? _____

_____

- -

❺ Soil All Around

1. Name some places where you have seen soil.

_____

_____

2. What kinds of things are usually found in and around soil?

_____

_____

3. What do you think is in soil? Name all the different things.

_____

_____

❻ Looking at Soil

1. Pour each soil sample onto a sheet of newspaper. Use a hand lens to look carefully at each pile of soil.

2. How are the two soils alike? How are they different? Record your observations on the chart.

Soil A	Soil B

- -

❼ Soil Layers (1)

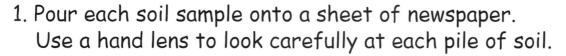

1. Put about a tablespoon of Soil A into a tube. Pour water into the tube up to about 1 inch from the top. Cap the tube.

2. Do the same with another tube and Soil B.

3. Shake the tubes for 1 minute. Then set them down.

4. Look at them the next day. What has happened to the soils?

_____

_____

5. On page 8, draw what you see in each tube.

❽ Soil Layers (2)

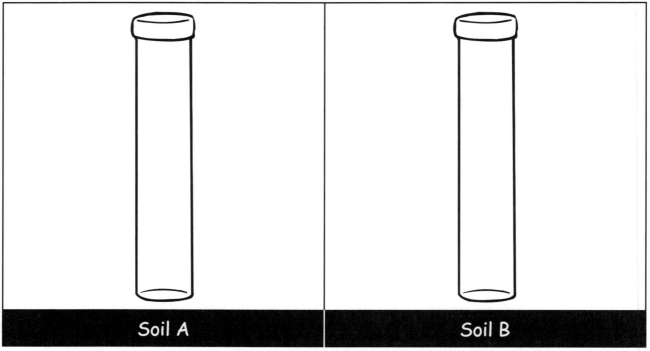

Soil A | Soil B

- -

❾ Weathering

1. Review pages 6–8. What are the main parts of soil?

_____

_____

2. Rub the two pieces of sandstone together over a piece of black paper.

3. What do you see on the paper? _____

4. Where do you think the small pieces of rock in soil come from?

_____

_____

⑩ Soil Humus

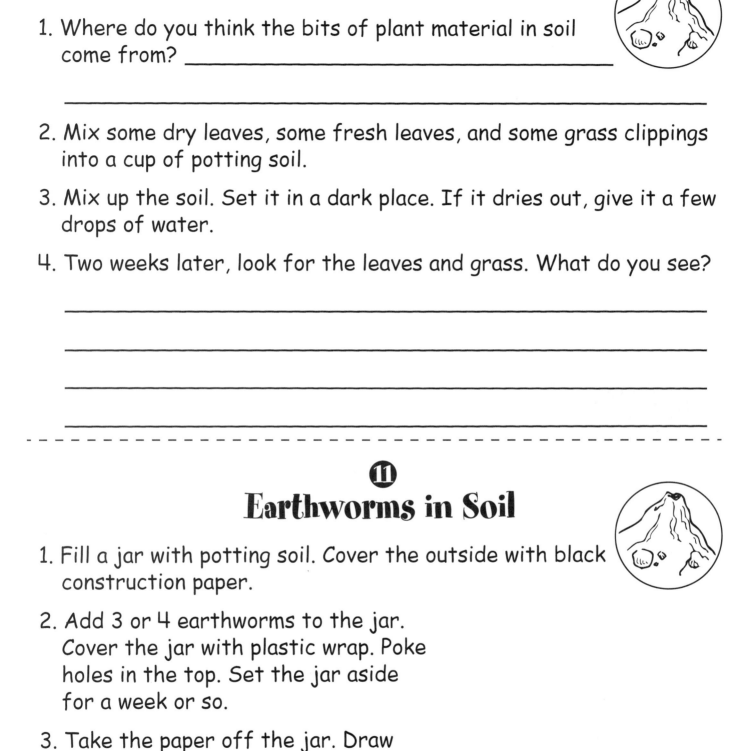

1. Where do you think the bits of plant material in soil come from? _____

   _____

2. Mix some dry leaves, some fresh leaves, and some grass clippings into a cup of potting soil.

3. Mix up the soil. Set it in a dark place. If it dries out, give it a few drops of water.

4. Two weeks later, look for the leaves and grass. What do you see?

   _____

   _____

   _____

   _____

⑪ Earthworms in Soil

1. Fill a jar with potting soil. Cover the outside with black construction paper.

2. Add 3 or 4 earthworms to the jar. Cover the jar with plastic wrap. Poke holes in the top. Set the jar aside for a week or so.

3. Take the paper off the jar. Draw what you see in the jar.

4. What do earthworms do to soil? _____

   _____

Light

Materials

- lab book pages 172–177, reproduced and fashioned into a booklet, one per student

- page 171, reproduced as an overhead transparency

- books

- pocket mirrors

- flashlights (small)

- spoons, shiny

- pencils

- plastic cups

- water

- eyeglasses

- large sheet of white paper

- glass jar

- prism

- small sheet of white paper

Objectives

- compare reflection of light by different objects, including mirrors

- determine that light bounces off mirrors at the same but opposite angle it came in at

- experiment with curved mirrors and the upside-down images they produce

- observe the effects of refraction

- examine eyeglasses and recognize how different lenses bend light to help people see

- experiment to determine the order of colors in the visible light spectrum

Preparation

Collect a number of pocket mirrors, or other small mirrors. Also collect a number of flashlights. Small ones with focused beams will work best. Find shiny spoons that show inverted reflections.

On pages 7 and 8, students will examine a pair of eyeglasses. In addition to those glasses worn by students in your class, you may want to collect additional pairs for examination. Try to find glasses with both convex (for farsighted people) and concave (for nearsighted people) lenses. Remind students that they must treat the glasses with the utmost care.

Practice the Colors of Light activities on pages 9–11. Locate a window and time of day where/when this trick will work.

Background Information

Light is a form of electromagnetic energy. It comes from the sun along with the other forms of EM energy (UV light, gamma rays, radio waves, etc.). Light travels in straight lines. Light rays bouncing off objects and into our eyes are what allow us to see the world around us. Without light, we cannot see.

When light strikes an object, it may be absorbed or reflected. Light reflects off an object at the same but opposite angle that it came in at. If the surface of the object is very smooth, like that of a mirror, all the light rays are reflected in a regular, parallel manner, and an image of the reflected object is formed.

Curved mirrors cause reflected light rays to cross over each other, producing an inverted image. Curved lenses also bend light rays, but unlike mirrors, lenses allow light to pass through them. A convex lens will cause light rays to converge on the other side of the lens. A concave lens will cause them to diverge.

White light is made up of all the colors of the rainbow. When combined, we see these as white light. A prism can be used to separate the colors of the visible spectrum. Since each color has its own wavelength, each bends at a different angle as it moves through the prism. Violet light is bent the most, while red light is bent the least. As a result, all six colors always appear in the same order.

Extension Ideas

Light energy can be used to cook food. A solar cooker concentrates solar energy into a small spot. Food placed in this spot will be heated by the collective solar energy. Have students make a solar cooker by covering one side of a sheet of flexible cardboard with the shiny side of aluminum foil. Bend the cardboard into a half-cylinder with the foil inside. Secure with a piece of string. Set the cooker in direct sunlight. Hold a marshmallow at the end of a long stick in the center of the cylinder (the hot spot). The marshmallow should begin to brown.

169

Page 1: 1) sunlight, fire, lightning, fireflies; 2) lamps (electric current passing through a filament), overhead lights (electric current running through a filament, or exciting particles in fluorescent lights), flares (chemicals).

Page 2: 1) It is dark; there is no light. 2) Answers will vary. Accept all responses. Then explain how light travels in rays from its source, spreading out in all directions. It strikes objects and bounces off them and then enters our eye. This is how we can see objects. 3) some summary of info just explained.

Page 3: Distribute a book, a mirror, and a flashlight to each student or group. 1) the book; 2) a slight reflection; 3) my face; 4) the light shining back out of the mirror. Explain that a mirror is a piece of glass with a shiny surface on the back. Light rays that hit the mirror are bounced off, or reflected. All objects reflect some light, but mirrors reflect all the light that strikes them, and they reflect it in a very orderly way. This is why mirrors can form images of objects placed in front of them.

Page 4: Distribute a mirror to each team of two. 3) The same distance away on the other side of the mirror, but still in front of it. 4) Light bounces off mirrors at the same angle it hits them, but in the opposite direction. Have students think about throwing a ball at a wall at an angle and how it would bounce off the same way.

Page 5: Give each student or group a spoon. 3) Both show a reflected image of my face. 4) The image in the spoon is upside down. 5) Answers will vary. Accept all responses. Lead students to understand that the curved surface causes the reflected light rays to cross over each other, creating an inverted image.

Page 6: Distribute a cup half full of water, an empty cup, and two identical pencils to each student or group. 3) The pencil in the glass with water will appear to be "broken." Also, the portion of the pencil submerged in the water will appear larger. Explain that this is because light travels at different speeds through air and water. So the light rays bouncing off the half-submerged pencil and entering our eyes are traveling at different speeds, and this makes it look like the two halves are located in different places.

Page 7: Distribute a pair of eyeglasses to each student or group. Call their attention to the lenses. 2) either "curved out" or "curved in."

Page 8: 1) either convex or concave; 2) either inward or outward; 3) Answers will vary depending on the eyeglasses.

Page 9: Make an overhead transparency of the art on page 171. Bring students to the area you have prepared. You will need a large sheet of white paper and a jar of water. 3) a rainbow of colors. Explain that white light is made up of all the colors of the rainbow. As white light passes through the water, each color is bent a different amount. So all the colors appear lined up next to one another.

Page 10: 2) red, orange, yellow, green, blue, indigo, violet

Page 11: Take students to the same sunny window location. Bring a prism and a small sheet of white paper. 2) rainbow of colors in this order: red, orange, yellow, green, blue, indigo, violet; 3) When white light is broken up, the colors of light always appear in the same order.

See page 170 "Page 9" for instructions on how to use the art on this page.

Colors of Light

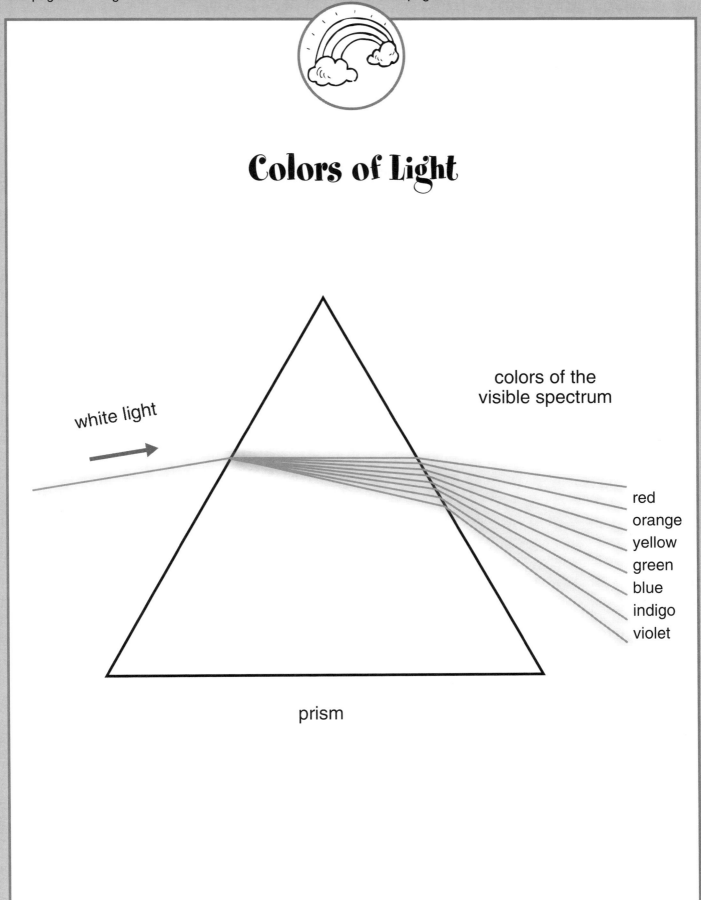

white light

colors of the
visible spectrum

red
orange
yellow
green
blue
indigo
violet

prism

171

My Lab Book

Light

Name _____ Date _____

---

①
Light Sources

1. Light is all around us. Think of some natural sources of light, even bursts of light that only last a second. Write your ideas below.

_____

_____

2. Now think of some manmade sources of light. How is the light made? Write your ideas below.

_____

_____

_____

❷
Seeing the Light

1. When you are lying in bed at night, why can't you see all the different things in your room?

_____

2. How do you think light helps you see?

_____

_____

3. Explain how light allows you to see.

_____

_____

_____

_____

- -

❸
Reflection

1. Hold a book up in front of your face. What do you see?

_____

2. Look in a window. What do you see?

_____

3. Look in a mirror. What do you see?

_____

4. Turn off the lights. Shine a flashlight in a mirror. What do you see?

_____

➍ Bouncing Light

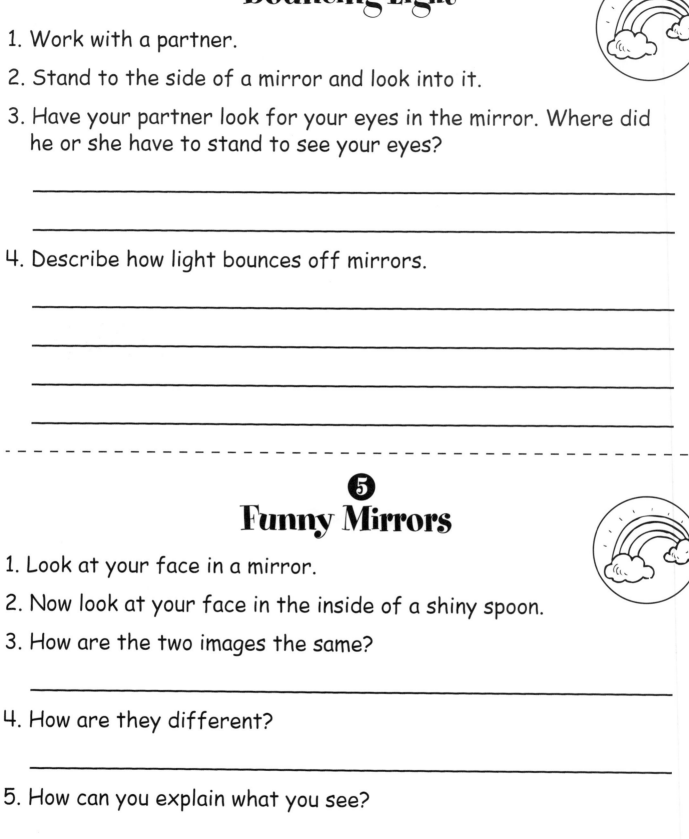

1. Work with a partner.

2. Stand to the side of a mirror and look into it.

3. Have your partner look for your eyes in the mirror. Where did he or she have to stand to see your eyes?

_____

_____

4. Describe how light bounces off mirrors.

_____

_____

_____

_____

- -

➎ Funny Mirrors

1. Look at your face in a mirror.

2. Now look at your face in the inside of a shiny spoon.

3. How are the two images the same?

_____

4. How are they different?

_____

5. How can you explain what you see?

_____

_____

❻ Refraction

1. Place one pencil in a cup half full of water. Place the other pencil in an empty cup.

2. Draw what the pencil looks like in each cup.

In Cup with Water	In Empty Cup

3. What difference do you notice?

_____

- -

❼ Lenses (1)

1. Examine a pair of eyeglasses. The clear plastic circles are called lenses. Lenses bend light that passes through them.

2. Look at the lenses of the eyeglasses. How would you describe their shape? _____

3. The diagram below shows how light rays are bent as they pass through two different kinds of lenses.

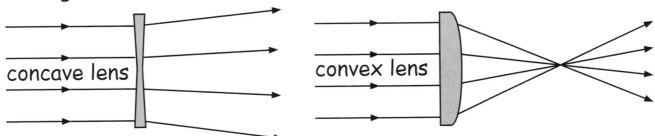

concave lens   convex lens

⑧ Lenses (2)

1. Which type of lens do the eyeglasses you are looking at have, convex or concave?

_____

2. How do these lenses bend light?

_____

_____

3. Convex lenses help people see up close. Concave lenses help people see far away.

4. Does the person whose glasses you have need help seeing near or far?

_____

- -

⑨ Colors of Light (1)

1. Place a large sheet of white paper on the floor in front of a sunny window.

2. Set a full jar of water on the window ledge. The jar should hang over the edge of the ledge a bit.

3. What do you see on the sheet of white paper?

_____

⑩ Colors of Light (2)

1. Draw the colors you see on the white paper in the order they appear.

2. In what order do the colors appear?

_____

- -

⑪ Colors of Light (3)

1. Hold a prism in front of the same sunny window. Have a partner hold a sheet of white paper a few feet from the prism.

2. Draw what you see on the paper.

3. Look back at page 10. What can you conclude about the colors of light? _____

Weather

Materials

- lab book pages 182–187, reproduced and fashioned into a booklet, one per student

- page 181, reproduced for each student

- page 61, reproduced for each student (Beaufort Scale in Air unit)

- outdoor thermometer

- windsock

- compass

- rain gauge

- barometer

Objectives

- identify atmospheric conditions that comprise the weather

- learn how to use weather instruments, including windsocks, thermometers, the Beaufort Wind Speed Scale, cloud charts, rain gauges, and barometers

- use new skills to record weather data for one or more weeks

- recognize that some weather conditions seem to be linked

Preparation

The first several lessons of the unit have students looking at individual weather factors. Plan to conduct these lessons on days when that factor is measurable. For example, conduct the wind speed lesson on a day when there is wind. Conduct the rain gauge lesson on a rainy day, and so on. Preview the lab book pages before planning your unit schedule.

You may choose to collect multiple instruments in some lessons so that students can get more familiar with them. Multiple outdoor thermometers, windsocks, compasses, and rain gauges might be beneficial.

Find an open area where students can measure wind direction and speed. An open playing field surrounded by trees is a good spot. Avoid corridors where wind might be funneled, giving an inaccurate result.

Review the cardinal directions of a compass face.

Locate a place on the school grounds to install the rain gauge. It should not be near a building where rain might run off and into the vessel. If you do not have one already, get a barometer and place it on the classroom wall.

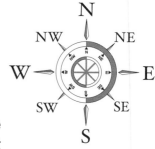

Note: Students will need five copies of the weather charts on lab book pages 10 and 11. After stapling the lab books together, instruct students to number the weather chart pages 10 through 14.

Background Information

When we talk about "the weather," we are really talking about a collection of atmospheric conditions, including air temperature, wind speed and direction, cloud cover and type, precipitation, and air pressure. None of these conditions is independent of the other. As one condition changes, so do the others.

Setting off the chain of events that define the weather is the sun. The sun heats Earth's surface, causing water to evaporate and rise. As cooler air rushes in to take its place, wind is created. As warm, moist air rises, it cools, condenses, and produces precipitation. Since air moves from areas of higher pressure to areas of lower pressure, differences in air pressure between regions can create movement of air and all that comes with it (precipitation, clouds).

Air temperature varies daily (according to the sun's schedule of rising and setting) and seasonally (according to the tilt of Earth in relation to the sun). In some places, rising temperatures are associated with impending rainfall as warm, moist air is drawn up into the atmosphere where it cools and releases its moisture.

Winds are named according to the direction from which they blow. This is because the origin of the wind, and the area it blows over on its way to a place, determine the nature of the wind (temperature, moisture level).

Extension Ideas

Have students use the World Wide Web to research weather conditions in a region completely unlike their own. What are the daily weather conditions in the Amazon rainforest? In Antarctica? Do they vary much day to day? Month to month?

179

Page 1: 1) Answers will vary. 2) temperature, clouds, wind, rain or snow, thunder and lightning; 3) Answers will vary, but students might mention that clouds and rain seem to be linked, or snow and temperature.

Page 2: 1) thermometer. Review the Thermometer transparency on page 51 with your class if you feel it's necessary. Thermometers must be placed in the shade. Direct-sun readings are inaccurate. 4) Students might mention time of day, time of year, cloud cover, and so on.

Page 3: Conduct this lesson on a day when the wind is blowing. Go over cardinal directions with students by drawing the image in the Preparation section on the board. 5) Students might suggest looking at how flags or trees are blowing.

Page 4: Give each student a copy of the Beaufort Wind Speed Scale. Take them outside to the designated area.

Page 5: Give each student a copy of the Cloud Types chart on page 181. Go outside with the class. Help them, as needed, to identify clouds they see, and to estimate total cloud coverage.

Page 6: Conduct this lesson on a rainy day. 1) Yes. Place the rain gauge in the designated area with the class. Check the gauge again the next day.

Page 7: Help students, as needed, to read the barometer. 2–3) If the air pressure is low, the weather is probably stormy or cloudy or windy. If the air pressure is high, the weather is probably clear and calm and sunny.

Page 8: If there is no change in air pressure the next day, wait until there is. Then conduct the lesson that day. 4) Students may note that falling air pressure brings stormy weather, while rising air pressure brings fairer weather.

Page 9: 3) Answers will vary. Encourage students to note links between air pressure and all other weather conditions, cloud cover and temperature, rainfall and cloud type, and so on.

Page 10: Have students collect data every day for 5 days. Add more Weather Chart pages if you want students to collect data for longer.

Cloud Types

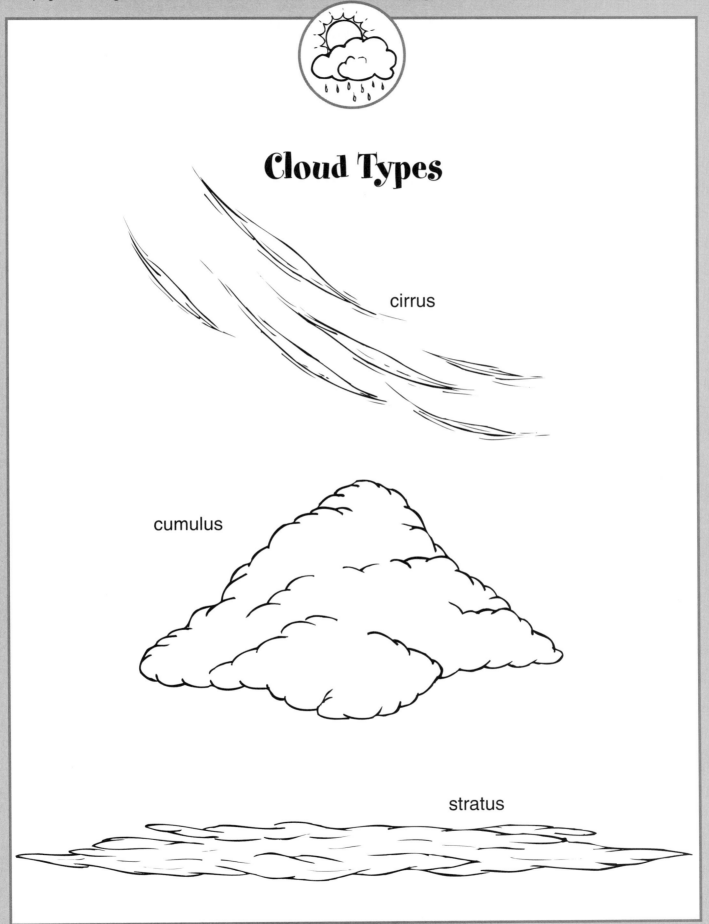

cirrus

cumulus

stratus

181

My Lab Book
Weather

Name _____ Date _____

- -

①
What Is Weather?

1. What's the weather like today?

_____

_____

2. Think about all the different things we mention when we talk about the weather. What are some of these things?

_____

_____

3. Do any of these things seem to be linked together? How?

_____

_____

❷ Temperature

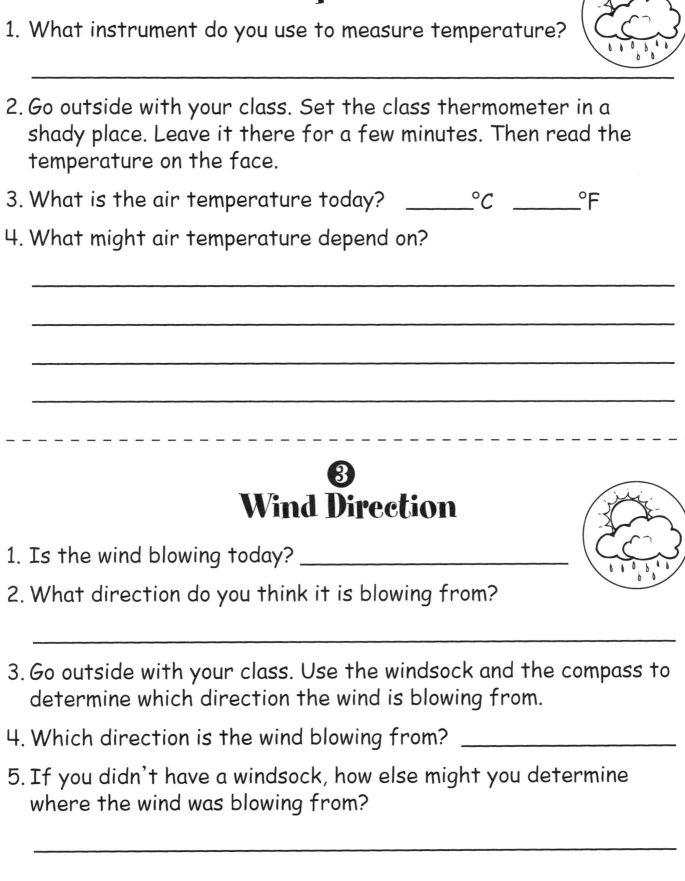

1. What instrument do you use to measure temperature?

_____

2. Go outside with your class. Set the class thermometer in a shady place. Leave it there for a few minutes. Then read the temperature on the face.

3. What is the air temperature today? _____°C _____°F

4. What might air temperature depend on?

_____

_____

_____

_____

- -

❸ Wind Direction

1. Is the wind blowing today? _____

2. What direction do you think it is blowing from?

_____

3. Go outside with your class. Use the windsock and the compass to determine which direction the wind is blowing from.

4. Which direction is the wind blowing from? _____

5. If you didn't have a windsock, how else might you determine where the wind was blowing from?

_____

_____

❹
Wind Speed

1. How would you rate the wind speed today on a scale of 1 to 12? _____

2. Go outside with your class. Use the Beaufort Wind Speed Scale to estimate the speed of the wind in kilometers per hour (kph).

3. What wind speed did you come up with? _____

4. What Beaufort Scale number did you come up with? _____

5. How close was your guess?

_____

_____

_____

- -

❺
Clouds

1. Go outside. Look up at the sky.

2. How much of the sky is covered by clouds?

    all   most   half   a little   none

3. Look at the cloud chart. Which of the clouds on the chart do you see in the sky? Describe all the different clouds you see and count how many of each.

_____

_____

_____

❻ Rain

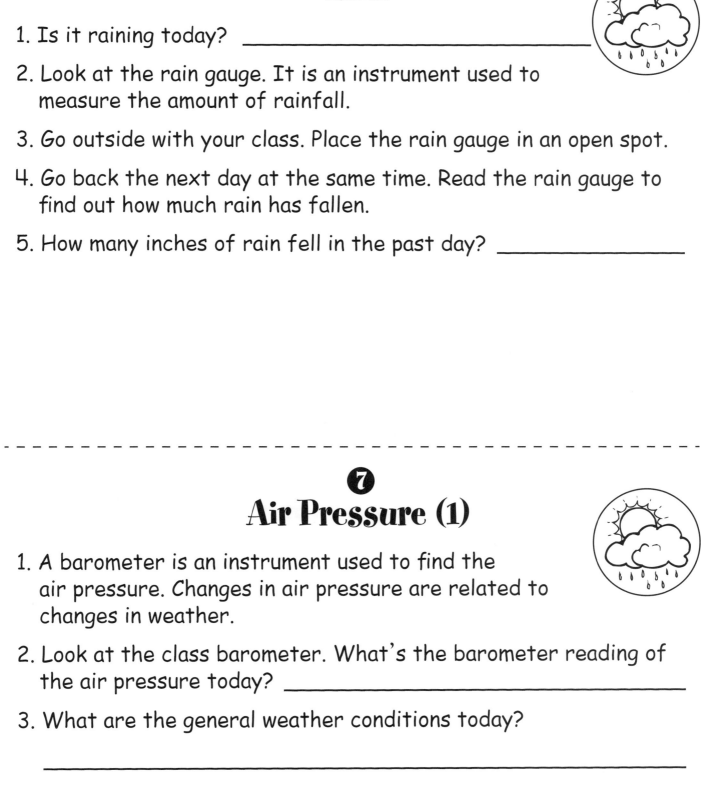

1. Is it raining today? _____

2. Look at the rain gauge. It is an instrument used to measure the amount of rainfall.

3. Go outside with your class. Place the rain gauge in an open spot.

4. Go back the next day at the same time. Read the rain gauge to find out how much rain has fallen.

5. How many inches of rain fell in the past day? _____

- -

❼ Air Pressure (1)

1. A barometer is an instrument used to find the air pressure. Changes in air pressure are related to changes in weather.

2. Look at the class barometer. What's the barometer reading of the air pressure today? _____

3. What are the general weather conditions today?

_____

_____

_____

⑧ Air Pressure (2)

1. Check the air pressure the next day.
   What is it? _____

2. Compared to yesterday, is the air pressure higher or lower?

   _____

3. What are the general weather conditions today?

   _____

   _____

4. What connection do you see between changes in air pressure and changes in the weather?

   _____

   _____

- -

⑨ Weather Watch

1. Use all the skills you have learned to collect weather data every day for a week. Use the charts on the following pages to record the data.

2. What changes did you observe during the week?

   _____

   _____

3. What connection did you notice between temperature and wind speed, cloud cover and air pressure, and so on?

   _____

   _____

⑩ Weather Chart

Date: _____

	Data
Temperature (°C)	
Wind Direction	
Wind Speed (kph)	
Cloud Cover	
Cloud Type(s)	
Rainfall (in.)	
Air Pressure (millibars)	

---

⑪ Weather Chart

Date: _____

	Data
Temperature (°C)	
Wind Direction	
Wind Speed (kph)	
Cloud Cover	
Cloud Type(s)	
Rainfall (in.)	
Air Pressure (millibars)	

Chemistry

Materials

- lab book pages 191–197, reproduced and fashioned into a booklet, one per student
- baby food jars, with lids
- whipping cream
- popcorn kernels
- cooking oil
- test tubes
- aluminum foil
- test tube clamps
- candles
- matches
- safety goggles
- vinegar
- salt
- mustard
- plastic spoons
- sugar
- salt
- flour
- talcum powder
- plastic cups
- toothpicks
- water
- marshmallows
- sticks or skewers
- JELL-O gelatin dessert
- hot water
- mixing bowls
- wooden spoons
- steel wool
- plastic wrap
- measuring spoons
- baking soda
- cotton swabs
- lamp
- bleach
- rubber gloves
- droppers
- old cotton rags
- skim milk
- pot for cooking
- strainer
- scrap paper

Objectives

- observe a variety of physical changes and identify the agent of change
- observe a variety of chemical changes and identify the agent of change
- use an emulsifier to improve salad dressing
- experiment to determine which of four chemicals dissolve in water
- use experimental results to identify an acid
- use an acid to write a secret message and heat to reveal it
- observe the chemical reaction that bleach produces in cotton
- make homemade glue

Preparation

Collect a number of test tubes and test tube clamps. Also collect safety goggles for students to wear while handling the test tubes over a flame.

You will need access to a refrigerator (pages 7 and 8) and a stovetop or hot plate (page 13). Make arrangements as needed. You will also need a lamp with an exposed bulb (page 11).

Warn students to use extreme caution when working with open flame. They should always wear their safety goggles and pull back long hair. Also remind them to use caution when handling bleach.

Collect a number of old rags that students can use to experiment with the effects of bleach.

Background Information

Substances can undergo physical and chemical changes. Physical changes do not produce new substances. Chemical changes do. So melting butter, for instance, is a physical change, while burning paper is a chemical change. One way to distinguish between the two is to ask yourself if the change can be reversed. Physical changes can be reversed. Most chemical reactions cannot.

Heat is one common agent of physical and chemical changes alike. It can melt butter (physical change) and caramelize sugar (chemical change). Motion is another (stirring, shaking). Some chemicals react chemically when mixed. Bleach reacts with the dyes in clothing. Iron reacts with water and air to produce rust. Vinegar reacts with baking soda to produce carbon dioxide gas.

Lab Book Instructions & Answers

Page 1: Distribute a jar half full of whipping cream to each student or group. 1) It is a thick liquid. 3) It is fluffy, no longer a liquid. 4) It changed from liquid to semisolid. Shaking the cream back and forth.

Page 2: Distribute a corn kernel, a test tube with a drop of cooking oil in it, a small piece of foil, a test tube clamp, a candle, matches, and safety goggles to each student or group. 1) It is small, round, brown, and hard. 4) It popped. 5) It changed from small, round, brown, and hard to big, white, and fluffy. Heat caused the change.

Page 3: Give each student or group a jar and access to bottles of oil and vinegar, salt, and mustard. 2) The oil and vinegar don't mix well. 4) more mixed together; 5) They made the oil particles smaller, so they mixed with the vinegar better.

Page 4: Distribute a small amount of sugar, salt, flour, and talcum powder in plastic cups to each student or group. Also distribute four cups of water and a toothpick. 2) Sugar, salt, and flour dissolve; talcum powder does not.

Page 5: Distribute a small amount of sugar in a cup, a test tube, a test tube clamp, a candle, matches, and safety goggles to each student or group. 1) white and made up of individual crystals; 2) It melts and turns brown. 3) The sugar changed from white and individual crystals to brown and liquidy (then hardened). Heat caused the change.

Page 6: Distribute a marshmallow, a stick, a test tube, a test tube clamp, a candle, matches, and safety goggles to each student or group. 1) It is fluffy and white and soft. 2) It browns and gets hard on the outside. 3) In both cases, heat produced a chemical reaction that changed the sugar.

Page 7: Distribute one package of JELL-O, a mixing bowl, and a wooden spoon to each group. They will need access to hot and cold water. Have students follow the directions on the package. 1) It is a powder. 3) It is a hot liquid. 4) It is a cool liquid.

Page 8: Give each group their container of JELL-O. 2) It is a wiggly solid. 3) It turned from a powder to a liquid when I added hot water. It became a cooler liquid when I added cold water. It became a solid after it cooled in the refrigerator for several hours.

Page 9: Give each student or group a piece of steel wool in each of two cups, a piece of plastic wrap, and access to water. 1) gray; 3) The steel wool with water in its cup is rusting. The other one is not. 4) rusting; water and air caused the reaction.

Page 10: Distribute one cup of water and one cup of vinegar to each student or group. They will need access to the baking soda. 3) Water and baking soda produce no reaction. Vinegar and baking soda produce fizzing. 4) Vinegar is an acid. It reacted with baking soda to produce bubbles of gas.

Page 11: Give each student a cup of vinegar and a cotton swab.

Page 12: Prepare a dropper of bleach and a dropper of water for each student or group. Distribute the droppers in a plastic cup, along with rubber gloves and a piece of cloth. 3) The drops of bleach made the cloth white. The water just made it wet. 4) the bleach; it changed the color of the cloth.

Page 13: Heat 470 mL of skim milk mixed with 6 Tbsp. of vinegar until the milk curdles. Let the milk cool; strain off the curds. Mix the curds with 60 mL of water and a level tablespoon of baking soda. Mix. 3) glue; 5) glue.

My Lab Book
Chemistry

Name _____ Date _____

- -

❶
Creamy Delight

1. Look at your jar of cream. How would you describe the cream? _____

2. Shake the jar for several minutes. Now look at the cream.

3. Shake the jar for several more minutes. What does the cream look like now?

_____

4. Describe the physical change that the cream went through. What caused the change?

_____

_____

②
Hot Corn

1. Look at the corn kernel. How would you describe it?

_____

2. Put one corn kernel into the test tube with oil. Cover the tube with aluminum foil.

3. Use a clamp to hold the test tube over a candle flame.

4. What happens to the kernel after a few minutes?

_____

5. Describe the physical change that the kernel went through. What caused the change?

_____

_____

- -

③
Salad Dressing

1. Pour some oil into your jar. Now add some vinegar.

2. Shake the jar. Is there anything wrong with your salad dressing?

_____

3. Pour some vinegar into another jar. Add a pinch of salt and a bit of mustard. Shake the jar for a minute. Now add some oil. Shake again.

4. How does your salad dressing look now?

_____

5. How did the salt and mustard help?

_____

④ Dissolving

1. Use a hand lens to look at the four chemicals in front of you. Describe each one.

2. Mix each chemical into a cup of water and stir. Which ones dissolved?

Chemical	Description	Dissolves in Water?
1		
2		
3		
4		

- -

⑤ Heating Sugar

1. Look at the sugar in front of you. How would you describe it?

_____

2. Put some sugar in a test tube. Use a clamp to hold it over a candle flame. What happens to the sugar?

_____

3. Describe the chemical change the sugar went through and what caused it.

_____

_____

❻ Campfire

1. Look at your marshmallow. How would you describe it?

_____

_____

2. Put your marshmallow at the end of a stick. Hold the marshmallow over a candle flame. What happens to the marshmallow?

_____

_____

3. A marshmallow is made out of sugar. How is this activity connected to the activity you did on page 5?

_____

_____

- -

❼ JELL-O (1)

1. Look at the gelatin. How would you describe it?

_____

2. Pour the gelatin into a mixing bowl. Add the hot water and stir.

3. How would you describe the gelatin now?

_____

4. Now add the cold water and stir. How would you describe the gelatin now?

_____

5. Put the gelatin in the refrigerator for several hours.

⑧ JELL-O (2)

1. Take the gelatin out of the refrigerator. Scoop out some of the gelatin and hold it.

2. How would you describe the gelatin now?

   _____

   _____

3. Describe all the physical changes that the gelatin went through as you made the JELL-O.

   _____

   _____

   _____

- -

⑨ Metal and Water

1. Look at the steel wool. What color is it? _____

2. Add about a teaspoon of water to one cup. Cover the other cup with plastic wrap. Let the cups sit for several days.

3. What changes do you notice in the cups?

   _____

4. Describe the chemical change that took place in the cup and what caused it.

   _____

⑩ Acids in Action

1. Look at the two cups in front of you. One contains water. The other contains vinegar.

2. Pour a small amount of baking soda into each cup.

3. Describe what happens in each cup.

water: _____

vinegar: _____

4. Acids react with baking soda to produce bubbles of gas. Which liquid do you think is an acid, water or vinegar? How do you know?

_____

_____

_____

- -

⑪ Secret Message

1. Use a cotton swab and vinegar to write a secret message below.

2. Have your partner hold the message over a hot light bulb. Could he or she read it? What did your partner's message say?

_____

_____

⑫ Bleach

1. Put on rubber gloves. Be careful not to spill bleach on your clothes.

2. Put a few drops of water on one part of the cloth. Put a few drops of bleach on another part.

3. What happened to the cloth?

_____

_____

4. Which liquid created a chemical reaction in the cloth? What evidence do you have?

_____

_____

_____

- -

⑬ Ooey Gooey

1. Watch as your teacher curdles the milk and separates the curds.

2. Once the curds are dry, your teacher will stir in baking soda and water.

3. What does this stuff look like to you? Does it remind you of anything?

_____

4. Rub some of it on a piece of scrap paper. Fold the paper over and leave it for a few minutes. Then try to unfold it.

5. What is the stuff you made? _____

Microorganisms

Materials

- lab book pages 202–207, reproduced and fashioned into a booklet, one per student
- page 201, reproduced as an overhead transparency
- potatoes
- self-locking plastic bags, small
- permanent ink markers
- assorted food scraps
- paper towels
- water
- hand lenses
- active dry yeast, packages
- plastic cups
- sugar
- toothpicks
- bananas
- organic potting soil
- grass clippings
- decaying leaves
- small plastic garbage can
- pond water
- petri dishes

Objectives

- make predictions about where microorganisms might live and what they might need to survive
- observe bacterial colonies growing on a potato that students contaminated with their hands
- compare molds growing on different types of food
- experiment to determine what yeast needs to grow and be active
- recognize that yeast is a decomposer
- recognize that soil contains lots of microorganisms
- construct a class compost pile and observe the effects of microbial action on food and garden waste
- observe microorganisms living in pond water

Preparation

Slice the potatoes into ½-inch thick slices. Blanch them in boiling water for 1 minute.

Collect a wide variety of fruit and vegetable scraps. (Do *not* collect meat scraps or eggs.) Also collect scraps of bread made without preservatives and small pieces of cheese.

Locate a place where students can leave their plastic bags of food scraps and wait for them to develop mold. Mold grows best in warm, dark environments.

Obtain a small plastic garbage can (or similar container). Poke holes all over the container and its lid to allow air circulation. You will use the container to make a class compost pile. The container should be kept outside in an unexposed area.

You will need to collect a jar of pond water. (If you do not have a pond nearby, visit a local pet shop and tell them the microorganisms you are looking for.) Collect water near the vegetation at the edge of the pond. Look for daphnia and other small organisms floating about.

Background Information

Some of the microorganisms most familiar to us include mold, yeast, bacteria, and plankton (small plant- and animal-like organisms that live in water and form the bottom of the food chain). Many microorganisms cause spoilage and disease. But we also depend on microorganisms for many different things (making cheese and yogurt, antibiotics, decomposition, digestion).

Soil contains a number of microorganisms. Without them, dead plant and animal material and waste would simply collect on the ground and never be broken down into bits small enough to be used again by new plants. A compost pile is a layered heap of food and garden scraps mixed with microbe-containing soil, some water, and air. The microbes break down the scraps, making rich soil.

Lab Book Instructions & Answers

Page 1: 1) tiny plants and animals (and other organisms that are not classified as plants or animals); 2) Answers will vary, but students might mention moldy food, colds they've had, mildew in the shower, etc. 3) food, water, a place to live, light.

Page 2: 1) Students may know that their hands can carry microorganisms that can make them sick if ingested. Pass out a potato slice and a resealable bag to each student. Have them label their contaminated bag "Unwashed." After they wash their hands, give them another potato slice and bag. Have them label this bag "Washed." 4) The "unwashed" slice is turning sort of black or has something growing on it.

Page 3: 2) Answers will vary, but might include bread, cheese, fruits, and vegetables. Distribute paper towels, plastic bags, and food scraps. Have students prepare their bags and label the bags with the food they contain.

Page 4: 1) It probably looks gross, with fuzzy stuff growing on it. 2) Students should draw what the mold looks like. Make sure they note the spore cases (stalks with balls) and the color of the mold.

Page 5: 2) No, they have different colors and shapes.

Page 6: Distribute a plastic cup with ½ package of yeast in it to each student or group. 1) Students may or may not recognize the yeast. Encourage them to smell the yeast to help identify it. 2) Students may guess food and water. 3) Encourage creativity. Supply students with whatever they need within reason.

Page 7: Distribute a fresh cup of yeast to each student or group. They will need access to the warm water (110°F) and the sugar. Make sure the water is at the right temperature when students add it to their cups. 3) The yeast is starting to grow and bubble and smell strong. 4) Help students conclude that yeast needs warmth and water and food. It also needs air.

Page 8: Distribute plastic bags, pens, bananas, and yeast to each student or group. 4) The bag with yeast is much grosser than the other bag. More decomposition is going on in the "Yeast" bag than in the "No Yeast" bag. Explain that yeast is a decomposer. Decomposers break down the dead bodies and wastes of larger plants and animals.

Page 9: 1) Students may recall that soil contains bits of dead plants and animals and animal wastes, so they may guess that microorganisms live there, too. Distribute plastic bags, pens, bananas, and soil to each student or group. 5) the "Soil" bag; Explain that soil contains microorganisms that act as decomposers, breaking down the bits of plant and animal material and returning the nutrients to the soil to make the soil richer.

Page 10: Show students the plastic container with holes. Layer soil, shredded food scraps, grass clippings, and decaying leaves in the container. Sprinkle some water between each layer. 2) food scraps, grass, leaves, water; 3) It is made up of distinct layers. Two weeks after you make the compost pile, use a small shovel to turn over the layers. 4) The layers have disappeared and it looks like rich soil. Remind students that many microorganisms are decomposers. The microbes broke down the food, grass, and leaves into bits so small you can hardly see them. They are now part of the soil. They make the soil rich.

Page 11: Make an overhead transparency of Pond Microorganisms on page 201. Place a few tablespoons of pond water in a petri dish. Each student or group will need one dish. They will also need a hand lens. 1) Probably nothing much. Maybe bits of floating plants. 2) Students may see some of the microorganisms shown in the transparency. Show them the transparency. Explain that larger pond organisms feed on these microorganisms. Introduce the concept of a food chain.

See page 200 "Page 11" for instructions on how to use the art on this page.

Pond Microorganisms

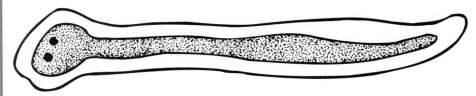

planaria

 stentor

 volvox

 amoeba

 blepharisma

 paramecium

 rotifer

 stylonychia

 vorticella

 euglena

hydra

daphnia

201

My Lab Book

Microorganisms

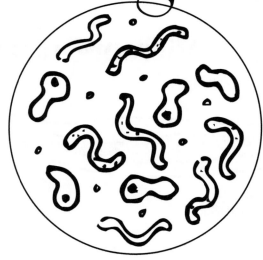

Name _____   Date _____

- -

❶
What Are Microorganisms?

1. Micro- means "tiny," and organisms are things that are alive. So what are microorganisms?

_____

2. Where might microorganisms live? Think about some experiences you might have had with microorganisms.

_____

3. What do you think microorganisms need to survive? (Hint: Think about some of the things you need to survive.)

_____

❷ Wash Up!

1. Why do you think your mom tells you to wash your hands before dinner?

_____

2. Wipe your fingers on the potato slice your teacher gives you. Then put it in the plastic bag and seal it.

3. Wash you hands with soap and water. Touch the other potato slice and put it in the other plastic bag.

4. A few days later, look at both bags. What do you see?

_____

_____

_____

- -

❸ Comparing Mold (1)

1. Mold that grows on food is a kind of microorganism.

2. What kinds of foods have you seen mold growing on?

_____

_____

3. Put a damp paper towel in a plastic bag.

4. Choose one kind of food scrap and put it in the bag. Seal the bag, leaving some air inside.

5. Put the bag in a warm, dark place for several days.

④ Comparing Mold (2)

1. Look at the food scrap you put in the bag a few days ago. Does it look different? How so?

_____

_____

2. Use a hand lens to look closely at the food. Draw what you see.

Type of Food:

- -

⑤ Comparing Mold (3)

1. Look at some of the bags your classmates prepared. Examine them with a hand lens. Draw what you see.

Type of Food:	Type of Food:	Type of Food:

2. Do all the molds look the same? If not, how are they different?

_____

_____

❻ Growing Yeast (1)

1. Look at the tiny gray balls in the cup. What do you think they are?

   _____

2. These tiny balls are yeast. Yeast is a microorganism. Right now, the yeast is not active. It needs a few things to wake up and start growing. What do you think those things might be?

   _____

   _____

3. Add the things you named to the cup. Watch it for several minutes. Does the yeast come alive? Describe what you see and smell. _____

   _____

- -

❼ Growing Yeast (2)

1. To your new cup of yeast, add a tablespoon of warm water and a teaspoon of sugar. Stir gently with a toothpick.

2. Let the cup sit for several minutes.

3. What do you see happening in the cup?

   _____

4. What does yeast need to grow and be active?

   _____

   _____

❽ Yeast Feast

1. Label one plastic bag "Yeast" and the other "No Yeast."

2. Put a few slices of mashed banana in each bag. Sprinkle some yeast into the bag labeled "Yeast." Seal the bags, leaving some air inside.

3. Leave the bags in a warm, dark place for several days.

4. What differences do you notice between the bags after several days?

_____

_____

_____

_____

- -

❾ Soil Surprise

1. Think about how soil is formed. Do you think that soil contains microorganisms? Explain.

_____

_____

2. Label one plastic bag "Soil" and the other "No Soil."

3. Put a few slices of mashed banana in each bag. Sprinkle some soil into the bag labeled "Soil." Seal the bags, leaving some air inside.

4. Put the bags in a warm, dark place. Look at them every day.

5. Which bag has mold in it first? _____

⑩ Compost Pile

1. Follow your teacher's directions to make a class compost pile.

2. What kinds of things went into the compost pile?

_____

_____

3. Describe the compost pile the day you made it.

_____

_____

4. Describe the compost pile two weeks later.

_____

_____

- -

⑪ Pond Alive

1. Look at the pond water you or your teacher collected. What do you see?

_____

2. Now use a hand lens to look at the water. Draw and describe what you see.

_____

_____